Greatest Caring Secrets Revealed

As Promised

Francis Epulani

authorHOUSE®

AuthorHouse™ UK Ltd.
500 Avebury Boulevard
Central Milton Keynes, MK9 2BE
www.authorhouse.co.uk
Phone: 08001974150

First published by AuthorHouse 5/24/2011

ISBN: 978-1-4490-6468-6 (sc)

Acknowledgements

I must pay my sincere tribute to my late mum, Viridiana Manyoni, who left this life on 23/10/2009, the same day I finished this manuscript. She was in a geographical location far removed physically from I, and I could not hear her last words. Mum, I still love you, and shall love you always. Give Dad, Jervas, and Donald, my beloved brothers, my love, and do please keep walking with me. Heartbroken, I still worked on so that your love would flow onto everyone reading this book.

I am grateful to all the children in care, present and past children in care, represented by Taxina, for letting me tell their stories; children who trusted me as their tutor, all childcare providers, foster parents, and fellow teachers who allowed me their best practice secrets.

Many people shared their views on children in care, and if I did not mention them, I still am grateful for their input.

I am particularly grateful to Moses Muwamba Banda, Victor Kaitell, and Kathy-Mark Evans for critiquing the manuscript; to Sally-Ann and Anne-Marie for their convivial support; to Tendai Kambeu, Sam Couser, and Elijah Chiriseri for their ongoing support; and to Anna Pamula for kindly modelling for the book cover.

I am equally indebted to emeritus professor Dr Thomas Kutsch, Bonn/Koln, as he has been my ever-present inspiration.

Most of all, to my children: Deus Nathan, Tamara, Moses, Dalitso, and my dear wife Malangizo, who still believed in me, even when I stole family time to write this book.

Dedication

This book is dedicated to all the children in care, to their carers, to their teachers, to whomever bends backwards to love these kids, and to carers who suffer accusations, allegations, and domestic unhappiness for helping other people's children.

CONTENTS

Preface

This book is written based on reality. The names have been changed, as have the sequence of events, and description of places. It is meant to reflect the way I have been seeing life in care, as a looked-after child. As the book is written in first person voice, any ideas that appear similar to some publication, unless directly referred to, were not intended.

It has therefore been written in the order I chose. Each letter needs to be read as independent of the others. Therefore, no conflict of facts exists as in real life we always choose what and how much to tell one person and what and how to tell another one. I write as I would talk to various people depending on how I am related to them. Similarly, if everything came out in the expected order, "boring" would have been the one best description for this life.

As the book comes in the form of letters, some details may appear to be repeated in different chapters. This was deliberate, as the letters portray me talking to different people. This is because the message is going to different people who may receive it differently depending on their roles, responsibility, and even whether they have children of their own or not.

Any offence that may be caused to any parties is unintentional, as are any similarities to real life people. The solutions suggested about the plight of looked-after-children are real. Just as the one who wears the shoes knows where they pinch, these solutions, while practical to current and past children in care, may not be the institution's version or what bosses would necessarily agree with. After all, most bosses never stoop down to a child's height. Is it any wonder that they make outlandishly monstrous decisions on the basis of third-party reports?

It is my hope that many children, youths, most of the people who matter in the life of any child, and those who have been entrusted with making decisions for our communities shall join me on the journey through these secrets.

As you are reading this book, this very minute, some child is on the fence, sitting in a corner or even at a bus stop, wishing someone understood them and would make a difference in their life. They are looking for a friend. Could that someone be you? Well, welcome to my world.

Shed loads of Love,

Taxina (and Doctor Francis S. Epulani, 27.10.2009)

www.greatestcaringsecrets.com

CHAPTER 1

Welcome to City Invisible

Candle Mews,
Radnor-cliff Crescent,
Folkston,
CT20 2JQ

Today's date

Dear Visitor,

My name is Taxina. Others call me Taxine. My dad and close friends call me Taxie. So you too can call me Taxie.

Still green, just turning fifteen, I am probably younger than you imagined. I am one of the many teens, younger or older, who are in some way looked after. I am one of those children brimming with love, one of those children you may want to foster.

There are many children like me. Some of us have lost one parent or the other. Some of our parents killed themselves through drug abuse or even suicide. Some parents died in war, and others were killed by drug gangs. Yet others died emotionally in that they forgot their roles as parents and think we children are nothing but bores and chores. Yet others gave up on us, failing to cope, becoming overwhelmed by life. They sought solace in a boat of fame, limelight, and glamour, and soon, they floundered on life's shores.

Many adults say that I am an ever angry person. They say that I create a smoke screen when talking to them. I have learned to accept that few people really know me. I am a broken young person, a young soul that has been shown nothing better than a self destructive way of living. But I am a hopeful young soul seeking lasting and loving solutions.

Children like me do not have a real world (you shall soon understand how and why). Actually, not many people know the truth about us. We, each thrive in an imaginary world, and speaking for many, I say that Invisible City is where we live and grow.

While I am writing these letters from a home by the sea in Folkestone, I shall take you by the hand and show you around my world. I shall do this by opening my inner thoughts and secrets to the different people that have come into my life.

Therefore, if you ever wanted to foster a child, or you are a young person who wants to prosper in care, or even a parent who fears for the future of your child, come and take a peep at my secrets.

For the first time ever, you shall be let into the realities, positive lessons from what I observed, and tips on how the ever important machinery of "looked after children" can really work. You therefore can be sure that I am not shooting from the hip.

We are mostly standing on one leg, and we are getting good at it too. Every day, we are looking forward to new surprises as some placement breaks down for some poor member of our group.

So if you are brimming with love like we are, or you want to find a warm heart to make your world meaningful, if you would gladly end some child's endless displacement, please do come in. You have love to give out? Well, may we have some, please? As for us, we have love in drums, even though we may be portrayed as mean and challenging, we have shed loads of love for you. Do please come with me into our world.

Love Taxie XXX

CHAPTER 2

Did I hear you ask, "Who are these children?"

Candle Mews,
Radnor-cliff crescent
Folkestone,
CT20 2JQ

Today's date

Dear Settled Family,

I overheard you talking to our head of care and asking, "Who are these children and why are they here?" We are what you see as young boys and young girls out to play, out to have fun, messing about, and at times, looking and creating trouble for adults. But that is not the complete story. We are generally socially invisible young men and women, invisible girls and boys. Yes, socially invisible children that some group of society is trying to reshape into honest hopeful individuals with a future.

The various social forces, the position and direction taken by our rulers of the day, affect individuals. Those individuals' reaction impacts families and their members. The ultimate frustrations of the adult social environment get offloaded somewhere else, onto some easy targets. You guessed right who: "looked after children."

As in most of my letters, I pose questions to express my feelings. Here is a test. You certainly have seen or heard about road rage, drivers chasing each other. Have you ever thought about the possible effect the drivers' chases and possible fights can have? They can put some innocent child into care. Or how ministers' greed, saving money to pay for endless wars, wars they never win and yet cutting funding from children services while they thousands of pounds for bogus expenses, leads to an increase in taxes as well as prices? How this can make families suffering hardship release their anger on innocent little ones at the slightest provocation?

Are we loved and wanted? Sometimes I doubt it, as our birth is encouraged to support the future needs of the many aging people who cannot work anymore. Are we just goods to ensure income to manage others in their retirement?

Those decisions, rules, or policies-whatever you adults call them - ultimately translate into a child being persecuted by the society he or she never chose to be born into. The slightly lucky ones end up in care, the supposed haven that sometimes isn't. We do honestly hope that none of your children or relatives' children shall have any need to ever come or be brought here.

Being in care is a definite sign of hope for any young person who has been let down by society. It can be fun, having the entire day planned for you. I have to wake up by at least seven o'clock on week days and have a wash or shower if I want. More often, even the day of having a shower is fixed. There is some arrangement for education, either in a conventional school, mostly comprehensive and almost never a grammar school.

We have set meal times and some chores to which we can say no and get away with it, in most places.

Smoking is frowned upon but not actively discouraged.

We have plenty of fun, but sometimes our days are too structured to have spontaneity. It then stops being fun. For example, one day I only said "I wish I went horse riding" to my carer. The next three months I had two weekly horse rides paid for. Similarly we can go for discos every fortnight and have real night out clothes purchased. To do all these things, taxis are hired for us. Actually we never have hard cash to spend loosely. There are times when I get so skint that I ask the manager for permission to wash my carers' cars for a fiver each.

It is when I tell some friends at school about my designer clothes that I realised it is a far cry beyond the real world for real families. I realised that my little sister, staying with Mum, can ill afford any of these. Yet she enjoys the freedom of a bird, with spontaneous laughter. All innocent fun is accepted as therapeutic and so many a celebrity fashion does not bypass us in care.

Can you think of a better place where one can enjoy such indulgences? Would you not think that this is where future millionaires are made? After all, we already practice spending money like young millionaires.

Yet we can be just as naughty and mess about like any other children. The major difference is that society often forces many of us to lose our innocence prematurely. That sums it all up for you.

Wait for it. In reality, it is an endless reminder of what a callous, cold, and double-faced world a child can be brought into through sheer greed, malice, ill will, senseless quest for fun, domination, illusory benefit schemes, and extreme materialistic lifestyles.

When I need someone to take me through the confusing past and find a way forward, everyone sees the wood and not the trees. I only get a reputation that blocks any future assistance and engagement from the significant others of adult society.

In the few instances when I met someone who allowed me to let my hair down, who ignored my whines but drew my smiles out, I promised that someday I would talk. I said that someday I would write heartfelt messages and letters to all who have mattered and still matter to me. I would open up to you all and show you the world you have never, and may never, experience.

As promised, welcome to my world. Enter with excitement, for this may be an emotional journey. Wear your armour, for it may be a bumpy journey that shakes your cool. It may move you beyond your zone of comfort and challenge the status quo. My trail has been one of tears, a future of fear, and sporadic chance meetings with individuals that inspire me to move on and follow the faint light to some end. As promised, I want to talk to you and let you into my life.

Every day that I lived in care, I asked some questions, noted practices, and kept secrets. At the time, no one seemed to want to listen to a teeny-weeny. So I kept my secrets, secrets that may make other children's lives a discovery holiday and listening adults expert parents. You are my significant other. Will you please come with me, sit still, suspend your judgement, and let me show you my world?

Yes, just as my friend Sara wrote to me, from Arundel Unit, a mental hospital, that paperwork kills patients in care and procedures ruin children's futures. If procedures kill children's futures, inadequately trained staff—social workers who cannot be social—make the children's coffins.

So welcome to my secret world. I reveal my secrets through letters to a variety of people, some of whom changed my life positively, and others whom I was pleased to see leave. Hence, keep your ears and eyes open as you read or listen to my letters, for there is a message especially for you. So there is no paperwork today. Let's just talk. As promised, here are the secrets I kept for you with shed loads of Love.

Taxina XXX

Faith is a bird that feels the light when the dawn is dark.

Rabindrath Tagore (Indian poet)

CHAPTER 3

Can We Please Join In?

Candle Mews,
Radnor-cliff crescent
Folkestone,
CT20 2JQ

Today's date

Dear Reverend Singsong,

My name is Taxina. I am as inquisitive as I am secretive. I have looked in society for someone who has time to observe human society, an active spectator who is looking for ways to make society better. Being not very familiar with the religion business, I did not really know you existed, let alone what you do.

This is because your big houses, which others call churches, only seem good for one to sit in and lose oneself in. This is all I remember other than some exciting music that I used to enjoy on the rare days when my mum took me to church. This was before she gave up on herself.

I have been troubled by a few questions that I need to find answers for to enable me to make sense of the next five years of my life. I have done my observations and put some of the questions to my carers but have not received crystal clear answers.

You will excuse me if this letter ends up reading a bit messy, as my brain is not in the best order at the moment. The paper may also look smudged with some red stuff. It is only nail polish as I have been painting my nails. I do not really want to go looking for cleaner sheets, as I may lose the thread of my thought.

Anyway, my first concerns are about your relationship to us Looked-After-Children or "LACs," as they call us. We call ourselves Children-In-Care, or "CHICs" for short. We love being called CHICs because it sounds cool. Do you have any slot in your heart or in your programme for children like us, who live outside any religion?

The other day, Marion, our cleaning lady, brought some piece of paper from her church. It had a summary of the sermon of that Sunday. More interestingly it had a list of activities that the church community had arranged for some of its youth, for whom it raised funds. It said that some of them would be going to Lourdes, France, and others to Assisi, Italy where some famous man was born or something like that. It also talked about a church choir, most of whose musicians were no older than thirteen. I hear that these youth also learn about creation and the meaning and purpose of mysterious life. Cool stuff, Mr Reverend Minister.

I immediately felt left out, much like if I had heard that my colleagues were going to Disneyland and I could not afford to go. Got the feeling? Am I not missing something? How come I have never heard about these things, neither have I been included in such activities? How does one join these groups? Do you have to be rich or belong to certain families to be allowed?

I also seem to have heard that you can never visit us, or are not allowed to visit any of us children, unless we or our biological families have been members of your religion, or we want you to.

But Reverend, considering that most of us are removed from our families following some trouble, sometimes abuse, how can anyone expect us to be practising members of any religion? Many of us fell out with our immediate family for one reason or another and either have been given up by them or have been forcibly taken away from them. They call it an "Interim Care Order" (ICO), you know. Don't ask me who orders the orderer! Others have no contact with their parents at all, as the parents failed them, or so we are told. How then can you expect these same 'failing parents' to have exposed us to any good religion?

Could it be that you have neglected us or, like everybody else, have already judged and condemned us as not worth the paper our names are written on?

Reverend Singsong, maybe you should visit us or send some of your young members to socialise with us, even for only a weekend. Let us see what your activities are about, what you believe, and maybe answer a few of our questions. Then, we can make our own minds up about what to believe, what to treasure, and what pass on to our own children if we get the chance.

I still have more to learn and shall be back to you soon.

Lots of Love,
Taxie XXX

CHAPTER 4

How Do You Make A Family?

Candle Mews,
Radnor-cliff crescent
Folkestone,
CT20 2JQ

Today's date

Dear Reverend Singsong,

As promised, I still need your guidance. How do you make a family? How do you prepare to do so, and for how long? Especially when you live in a children's home where all you see is people acting care roles that are dictated by the regulations and acts of parliament? Who does a young woman look up to for real-life models? And role models for life, not just role models in dressing, dieting, and applying makeup?

Who does a young man look up to for an accomplished father figure? Not just someone to show him how to tie a necktie, shave a beard, build six-pack muscles, or split wood. How does one become a good lover, husband, father, friend, and independent but respectable member of society?

Who does a young person look to and learn the secrets of having a happy lasting family when the media makes a circus of a family?

The media treat infidelities as pastimes and divorces and separations as spades for celebrities to dig gold off nosy audiences and magazine readers.

I remember one of my carers, Angela, saying that all celebrities are "big time life actors." But how is the poor child in a care home to know that they are acting? And that the ever-clean smooth faces are air brushed, and the clothes specially provided or rented? How does a child know where to draw the line between real, non-acting life and an imaginary life?

How do you become a respectable member of the society, on the right side of the fence, and yet have economic security enough to take your family for holidays without going into debt and enriching credit card companies?

These questions are not just from me, but also from some friends and colleagues I have known and lived with and others who left the care and foster homes just as I entered. I meet these people again and again through friends. I also developed questions after meeting some of these colleagues in a mental health hospital when I went with my mum to see one of her friends.

Titus, or "TT" as we fondly call him, is now 17 and did badly in his GCSEs. He has no real job and has had no lasting career, or vocational course, in spite of promises from social services people. Despite all the government statements, all the paperwork, all the money that the chair-people and their pen-pushers pay each other in the name of children-in-care, we, the youth in care, remain neglected in practice. We actually feel more neglected at a time when we most need some form of leaders to look up to.

While it is painful not to belong, the pain is acute for those of us in transition. Both the people at Monkey Tree (where Titus spends most of his spare time) and those at Mrs Clacton (his foster carer's) think Titus is a happy chappy and doing very well.

But they couldn't be more wrong. TT is worried sick. He has become more and more withdrawn over the last six months. He has seen happy families and met some children from such families, but he has not experienced any happy family himself.

Even looking back from the hostel where he now lives after leaving the foster home, he can still not recall of a home that did not seem to fake a relationship with him. Mentors seem to try very hard to make him feel accepted, but the more they try, the less personal the relationship becomes. It becomes clear that they are only fulfilling their job roles.

You see Reverend Singsong, the one thing we want is to be real humans, not the product of government papers. If anyone wants to love us, they just have to get on with it. They do not have to show extra effort. If we are off the path, then tell us off lovingly, and we shall get back to the path.

Titus, like the rest of us, could immediately feel that he would never be treated like the fosterer's own biological children. Sometimes the carers try to heap on us more favours than their own children receive. We resent that kind of behaviour as well. All we want is to be treated like other children. If moderation is good for others, it must be good for us.

Anyhow, Titus desires a job, independence, and a family of his own. At 17, with poor GCSEs faithfully dogging him, there is a lot of sudden movement—but without commitment—as everyone tries to enable him to settle down.

Titus told me the other week that as he was preparing to start life on his own, social workers were talking about the pathway or plan that would settle him down quickly. But when and where is the ground work? Titus tells me that he feels that he — or his now benefactors —seem to have missed some important part during the last two years.

But what is missing? Titus cannot pinpoint it. But a bit more discussion shows that, like many of us CHICs, Titus is an angry young person who feels short-changed by society. He does not think that he has received the best of support over the past thirteen to sixteen years.

These are our times of turmoil, these years in which GSCE prospects and results seem to spell our fate. They determine the legal support one can get, leading to academic, career, and employment success. Yet these are the years in which we feel unsure of who we are, where we are going, and if at all there is a future anywhere.

We are most confused, but at the same time, we are least willing to be told anything, let alone following advice. When else could a young person cry for more understanding, patience, and sympathetic leadership than at this time of searching for self identity? We have no clue regarding what we are searching for. Reverend Singsong, at what speed can one run, when one is determined to make progress, yet one is running down the wrong road?

Like Titus complained, creating pathways and designating personal advisers after seventeen years is too late. You may remember that I did ask you to visit us CHICs in our homes, even when we do not belong to your religion or church. At least given a glimpse of what others believe in, and having heard from several of you in time, at an early age, we may have something to stand by. Currently, we can fall for anything, and many of us already do.

Reverend Singsong, you are supposed to be the level-headed bearer of good news, like the good tidings we hear about in Christmas songs. Do we obtain some truth from you? Or do we live by some fictitious interpretation of our imaginary stories with which we fill our void?

We are fed up with people telling us what to do and what not to do without showing us any link to real life. You see, if you do not feel confident to visit us—maybe because you feel guilty about not having done enough to improve our lot in life—we shall understand. We would be more sympathetic because we expect more positive leadership from you. At least that is the impression we get from the little we hear and read about the likes of you.

Talking of leadership, Reverend, on the music TV programme, *The X Factor*, led by Simon Cowell, I do remember that we saw West Life, Beyonće, Whitney Houston, and even Mariah Carey. They were inspirational to the contestants. These were professionals adding to the contestants' regular mentors. I found their addition intriguing and uplifting as they had experience in the trade and could share a secret or two.

This got me thinking. Yes we are looked after children. But we also have dreams. We would dream even bigger if only we had real mentors at an early age, such as inspiring professionals from various walks of life. It would be nice to know professionals who have been in our shoes before. Reverend Singsong, would you please identify or look for such figures in society and negotiate with them to pay us a visit? Or encourage them to visit the nearest children's residence or foster home that they know of? Every adult out there was once a child and can identify with our emptiness.

We want to hear about the successes of others. What does it take to be where they are? How and when do we start? How do we rise above our current odds, (real, imaginary or attitudinal) such as the ever-growing anger we feel against the adult society? Surely there must be some lawyers, doctors, priests, inventors, government ministers, psychologists, and engineers out there who may have survived life in care.

We neither want their money (I admit I would not say no if they offered me a 500 quid!) nor graphic descriptions of their past abuse and tormented childhoods. We have enough misery of our own without adding theirs. We could use more heart-warming and encouraging stories. We know they have had frustrations (unless they were fostered by angels and were looked after by holy nuns), but that's not what we want to hear about. We want to know how they rose above their limitations.

Could they periodically visit some of us and keep us afloat with encouragement? We would know that they can speak our language and that they understand how short our fuses are. Or have they become so rich and grown so tall that they cannot even see the ground from which they came?

Maybe you can do better than plead with them. Give them a copy of my letter and let them make heads or tails of it. You will have played your part and it shall be up to them to hear our cry or plug their ears with cotton wool and look away from our tear-stained faces.

You see we fear the age of seventeen as much as employees fear retirement age.

What frustrates Titus is that help is seemingly coming at seventeen onwards, when no one tried enough to understand his cry for help in resolving his anger and teenage frustrations. Those frustrations interrupted his studies and he missed out on preparing for his GCSEs. He only managed to get one C in English, thanks to his escapism of reading too many novels and plays.

Now all talk from local authorities to helping him into adulthood seems late and misplaced. He tells me that they are to assess his needs, make him some pathway plan, and appoint him a personal advisor to lead him on his plan. The plan is about welfare, training, education, and some cash till he reaches 21 or finishes his education.

Well, Reverend Singsong, this sounds all very good. But I once heard that the road to hell is paved with good intentions. Forgive me if I am being cynical, but what good shall pathway plans, advisors, and cash handouts do for poor Titus? His low grades, at age 17, are below all reasonable entry requirements to some career education or training. Should he settle for the bare minimum training offered as a result of not having the proper grades?

It seems their solution creates an ongoing conflict with his ego and will surely knock his self esteem even lower. Another sorry product of some local authority care system or foster home! Do you now realise why we say that this help is rather belated?

It is all good for those lucky few who may have gone to such good schools as run by holy nuns, or those who managed to get into some grammar schools, bonded up with some brilliant team, and met teachers with insight. But the majority of us are none of those, and so our needs are critical before the age of 16. Lasting changes, like destructive habits, are grounded in our underlying behaviours. Most of us are emotionally tainted, and therefore, any talk of skills and instructions need to be emotionally cushioned.

I am not sure about the coming years, Reverend, but I do not think that I shall be any more emotionally charged and confused than in the past 14 to 17 years. Talk about me at 15. Now is when I need help, guidance, and an overbearing, patient advisor, with or without a pathway plan. By 16 many of us, particularly the girls, are too scared and damaged mentally to wait for these government advisors and pathway plans. We quickly set our sights on the shortcut to government benefits.

The other day I read about benefit-claiming teenage single mothers who suck up state resources and services. They do not work, but deliberately conceive to justify their benefits. The article, from the Christian Institute, I think, said only ten percent of teenage mothers stay with the fathers of their children. One in four mothers is now a lone parent as a chosen "lifestyle choice" to rely on state benefits instead of a male partner.

One Geoff Dench, who studies society, speaking regarding the British Social Attitudes survey, indicated that this is result of state benefits and handouts women can count on and not relationship breakdown. More of a state sponsored, chosen lifestyle. The government is replacing fathers and single mothers depend on benefits to bring up their children, which encourages young mothers "not to bother with male resident partners."

Similarly one Harriet Sergeant, speaking on her nine months exploration of the world of Britain's most disadvantaged youngsters, contended that single motherhood is "encouraged by the promise of benefits and rent-free accommodation."

Would you want a more revealing account than that of the Peckham housing estate drug dealer? When interviewed, he told Harriet that women became pregnant by a man they barely knew and received money from the government. Men are becoming eradicated "as the Government has taken [their] place." Yet we have grown up believing that marriage is the stable foundation of society? Little wonder this man has five children with different mothers. What real hope is there for those wretched little souls?

Do you now understand how unsupported we children in care are in regards to family values? Most of the articles in the daily paper point to the same sorry state:

> Quarter of mothers are single parents after being enticed by benefits 'lifestyle choice' (dailymail.co.uk, 25 February 2010)

> Young mothers reject full time work in favour of kids (christian. org.uk/news 19 February 2010)

> Boys lacking role models as state replaces fathers (24 September 2009 *christian.org.uk/news)*

> Fathers important, says Baby P report (dailymail.co.uk/news/ 13 March 2009)

> Marriage IS what matters most to family stability as only 3% of unmarried couples stay together until their child is 16 (dailymail. co.uk, 21 January 2010)

> Support marriage to combat family breakdown, says MP (christian.org/news 23 December 2009)

> Balls and Cameron clash on marriage (christian.org.uk/news 03 December 2009)

> 1 in 4 children suffer as cohabiting couples split (17 October 2008 christian.org.uk/news)

Even more formal, Harry Benson, of Bristol Community Family Trust, interpreted the findings of Britain's largest and most up-to-date family surveys (*Married and unmarried family breakdown: Key statistics explained*). He says that, regardless of age, ethnic group, benefit receipt, birth order, wealth or education, cohabiting parents are at least twice as likely to split up as married parents of similar income or education levels.

Reverend, feel for us girls. With a yapping and pooping baby, worse than that of Shrek and Fiona, how can you hold down a long term job, become a career woman, save for a pension, save for your own house, pursue higher education, or find a job that pays well? With no one to take the small person away, and give you fresh air to think in? I want none of that, but only if I can be helped in time to weather my teen transition.

That brings us back to Titus' original question: How do you make a successful family? There are no manuals and no real models for a child in care to learn from. How can you do a good job of running a family and providing for them?

Everyone talks about sex education, but in reality, they are talking about the biology of boys and girls, men and women. Do you really think that is helpful? No. Not when dogs can learn to do it from birth. What we really need help with is understanding of the associated feelings.

How can I convincingly tell someone I love him, but also want to have my boundaries respected, without fearing his rejection? I have learned the hard way that when girls want to look sexy and attract boys, we do not really mean to sleep with them. We only love the feeling of being praised, adored, or glamorised. We do not really want the emotional burden that comes with meeting their instant gratification or fighting to convince them to wait.

A long term relationship is what I would want, but often we are talking differently from boys. The most confusing thing is that boys really show that they adore a girl, but only up till they sleep with her. Thereafter they soon become lukewarm. She is no longer the one they claimed to want to walk the world for. She now has to fight to keep the boy's attention from looking at other new girls, which I guess are their next territories to conquer.

That makes me angry, Reverend. It does my head in, Reverend Singsong. It does. Honest.

Why do celebrities and the media ignore the emotional side of sex? That it involves a relationship, hurt feelings, and heartache?

Why do the Eastenders and Hollyoaks not show the boys that being a father is about continuously sharing the responsibility for a child for at least 17 years? That is what sex education should be about. Not just about hormones and physical anatomy.

Something beats me about teachers, yea. Teachers, and even some outspoken parents, claim to be teaching about life. But, no one prepares you for the pain of being dumped by someone who claimed they loved you. Why doesn't anyone tell you that this hurt is never halfway? That on a scale of 1 to 10, it always reaches a 10?

Let me admit to being both selfish and naughty as I have blames boys all the way. But hold on. That is not entirely true. The first time I mate Titus he did not want to interact with me at all. Somehow we got talking and he did mention to me that he may end up being a senior bachelor.

That made me laugh, although he was serious.

When I asked him why he said that, he intimated that he too had heartaches he was nursing, heart aches he had suffered in his early you when some redhead or ginger had let him down.

He admitted that there was nothing really physical involved, but that the girl appears to have known more than him about men and demanded something he did not understand. This was a girl he went to school with. Sadly he soon realised that she had turned her attention to another boy, much older than him. He reportedly got hurt by this girl calling him not manly enough. You see those scars are still raw, and I am sure that the girl has long forgotten having said that. So, boys can get hurt too?

How are we to learn to act responsibly when we are not exposed to the realities of sexually active teenage relationships? Reverend, I need answers, just does Titus and many other youths.

But before I forget, I meant to ask you for a solution to the plight of the likes of Delia. Delia is one CHIC who lives in the flats overlooking my mum's house. She is a typical Barbie girl, with who wears too much make up and puts on the same common place jeans and T shirts to grab attention from men. Delia lives a fast life that unfortunately seems to lead her nowhere. She has two children that are a year apart, and is now three months pregnant with the third, while her second born is only ten months old. She has two sauce pans, a coffee table, and a sofa settee that she scrounged from a charity shop. The settee is her bed as well as her chair. With the needs of her children, it means that the comfort of a mattress must come fifth on the list.

Delia proudly tells colleagues that she uses every trick in the book to get what she wants from men in exchange for what she has to offer. She even boasts of having registered on a numeracy course that provides free nursery care for the duration of the course.

Every morning she takes her two children to the nursery and proceeds to the course. But most of the days, she only attends half the time, claiming she feels unwell. In reality, she leaves to meet some respectable managerial clients that need lunch hour action. She does this in exchange for McDonald's takeaway that becomes dinner and breakfast for her and her children.

The other day, she even used her money from the dole to book herself a room for two at the nearest Travel Lodge Inn. Leaving the kids with her neighbour, she entertained four blokes that night (or so she told my mum), returning home in the wee hours of the morning.

Two of those blokes were partners of the neighbours she had lived with at her previous address. Yet Delia puts on such a convincing and reserved face that her failure to say no to men can be unbelievable to those who don't know her. But with her poor numeracy, no GCSEs, and only the easy-to-get council tax as her asset, how much can you blame her? What other option does Delia have?

My mum once asked Delia why she cannot space out her children, or even put off child-bearing for some years while she sorts her life out. But Delia realised that the only time the local authorities and health visitors attended to her needs was when she was pregnant and when her kids are young. She therefore decided to keep nursing a baby as long as it takes her to settle and furnish her flat. She hopes to create some savings for herself and her children this way.

Moreover, Delia does not know the fathers of her children. She believes that asking clients to use protection drives them away. What fate awaits her and her children? What fate awaits us all in a society where over half the children may come from the "Delias" of this world, as well as looked after boys and girls?

How could such youth mind their career training futures and ensure that they have a home before beginning to reproduce? Delia reports that local authorities helped her obtain her flat, gave her some basic cash, and without a real plan or understanding of how to survive the rest of her life, she was told, "Just get on with it!"

Yes, children must be seen and not heard. Children in foster homes are not even seen when foster mum have visitors or family functions. How can we learn to conduct social relations and at the same time prepare to live with someone all life long? Starting now, how can we resolve our burning grievances against society? Could you, please, give us some answers on these troublesome questions?

Well, Reverend Singsong, we are 'bovvered,' well and truly 'bovvered'!

The otherwise agile Titus is now visibly broken, and TT has a reason to be. He has self esteem and the manly macho feel, which are not supported by his impending future. Where does one begin planning one's future? When can one ever bring dreams into reality?

When I met TT last week, I could see that he wanted to talk. We each went into Lidl for a Coke and sat outside the library to drink. It soon appeared that we needed more peace, so we went into the public library. I have never seen so many books on so many different subjects! There were so many interesting books on how to do this and how to do that. Even on how to make one's own wine!

But guess what, Reverend Singsong? There were no books written on how to make a family. We even checked in their computer catalogue, which includes all books in every public library in Kent. We could not find a book about how to make and run a good family, how to be a good father, how to be a good mother, let alone how to be a good child. How can one know how to raise a happy family, how to raise happy intelligent smiling children, and how to avoid the bickering and poverty that makes junkies and suicidals out of beautiful innocent?

It is as if all authors were writing from a distance, watching and writing through hazy glasses. Some authors talked about the family and the society, but they did not address issues of identity, interpersonal relations, and interaction. No one addresses how we, CHICs can access emotional security without selling an arm and a leg. These are things we are struggling to make sense of in our transition.

Apparently, most authors do not understand our situations at all. I know this from the few books and articles I read and from some teachers and carers. To many of these people, children in care are either complete trouble makers or sweet angels waiting to be shown the way to some promised land after this troubled stay in the deserts.

Those of us who are sweet and sour, busy questioning our identity and status quo, and actively searching the way forward end up with labels. In searching for a lasting identity, we get paralysed into looking to someone else for validation of who we are. Others believe CHICs are the luckiest of children. In protest to that thinking Titus likes humming with Danny Hutton Hitters and Nik Kershaw lyrics:

> "Wouldn't it be good to be in your shoes?
> Even if it was for just a day,
> Wouldn't it be good if we could wish ourselves away?
> Wouldn't it be good to be on your side?
> The grass is always greener over there,
> Wouldn't it be good if we could live without a care?"

Yes, if people walked in our shoes, even if it was just one day, maybe they would understand the pain of not belonging, the tragedy of having no one to look up to as one's guide. This is why we turn to you, Reverend, someone who may have an understanding and a non-judgemental ear. At least you have some permanence; you're not going to be here today and gone tomorrow.

Well, I shall soon be back to you, Reverend. I need a strong coffee to wake me up.

Lots of love,
Taxie XX

CHAPTER 5

Then How Do You Make Lasting Friends?

Candle Mews,
Radnor-cliff crescent
Folkestone,
CT20 2JQ

Today's date

I have just finished my strongest coffee, Reverend. From the long talk with Titus, I started feeling like the Maggie of Don Williams, having had a dream to find a husband and be a wife. I rely on my iPod during a lonely afternoon playing the saddest tunes, as I stare at the flying planes above, wondering where they are going. Going beyond the scary age of 17, with nobody to go home to, "and it's almost time to close."

Do you now understand the fears and ways of thinking that torment girls in care by the ages of 14 to 16? I think that government intervention regarding advisors, path plans, and all that is perched in a wrong tree, on a branch uselessly higher than where the problem is.

My poor boyfriend, Greg, does not know the turmoil going on inside me. Too many times I doubt that we will be married ten years from now. He has a placid, calm background. I am a volatile nonentity, who secretly takes solace in weed, illicit snogs, and cuddles from men twice my age—men who caringly say, "Taxina, I love you. You are an innocent pretty young thing destined to break men's hearts," with a longing look in their eyes.

I never really want to be involved with them at all. Yet their lies seem to give me validation and value. It fulfils a strange yearning girls have.

I have a dream to be a happy mother, but not like the drug prone mother of mine, whose friends all come from pubs and rehabs.

I hear you say, "But you use weed?"

Wait. Three days ago, I asked Monica, the new community nurse, to bring me some nicotine patches and Niquitin mint gum. I started using them yesterday and will be a druggie no more, nor will I ever smoke again. So yes, I have been guilty of the same, but you can tell Santa that I am a good girl now. I deserve a sports car and some cheeky lingerie!

Dreaming of financial independence, I do not want to constantly look over my shoulder about crime; I want to be trustworthy and dependable. And the trouble is that, other than Angela—the former care worker whom I have only met in our home and do not really know in her own domestic life—I do not have any real role models. Not even from my own household. I have no models for how to be a good lover, good wife, and good mother.

You see, a bloke called DK was my dad's best friend. His name was Dean Kingsmeal, but Dad called him "DK." In school, friends mocked Dean, calling him "Kings' Dinner." He even had a few fights over the name. Dad, his closest friend from long before, invented the nickname DK and Dean accepted it. He liked it and now we still call him "Uncle DK."

Anyway, one day DK came home and took my sister and me to school. He first dropped my sister off and then me. Before I left his car, he told me that he had a surprise for me for that afternoon, which he would only show me if I behaved and worked very hard and passed my class work in school that day. I pleaded with him to tell me what the surprise was there and then, but he refused, kissed me good-bye, and drove away. Boy did that fire me up! I split my attention between listening to the teachers and dreaming about dinner or shopping in some expensive place. I couldn't wait to see whatever the secret surprise DK had for me.

At three, I could not wait to get out of class. DK's car smelled of chicken curry and made my mouth water. He had some Nandos piripiri chicken and chips in a carton with the all too clear pictures of golden brown fried chicken drumsticks. "Enjoy your lunch," he said, handing me the box and a bottle of fizzy water. "As soon as you have finished, we shall set going," DK said, popping a Britney Spears CD into the CD player. For some five minutes, we sat in sat in silence, me enjoying the take away, and he tucking into some computer technology magazine.

When I had finished, we set off for some mysterious place, as I had expected. But I was so anxious that I hardly noticed that it took us half an hour driving from Earls Court near Victoria Couch station to Belmarsh in Woolwich. I saw the letters stare at me: HM Prison, Belmarsh. That was a name I had heard about a year earlier, and a name my mother was not happy to mention. I wondered whatever it was we had to do or see here. How could Belmarsh have been a surprise, I wondered? Sure DK must have lost his marbles!

He turned to me and said, "We have come to see Don, your dad." Apparently he had already communicated with Dad because after the emptying of our pockets and top down search at the entrance, Dad was waiting for us in the visitors' lounge.

As soon as Dad saw me, he gave me a big warm hug, held my hand, and wept. He asked me how my little sister was, and I told him that she was okay, but ever annoying to me as usual. He told me that he loved me and my sister very much. Then, for a while, my dad acted like he would be choking on tears, but slowly he regained composure and kissed me on the cheek.

He said he would tell me a story that he hoped I would remember when I grew older and for the rest of my life. He told me the story of two women he had loved and trusted in his life, two women who had broken his heart into such small shatters that he was not sure about any future relations at all.

You know, Donald, my dad…, my dad, err, do excuse me if I stutter as thinking of this part always wells my eyes full of tears. It is one part of my history that I hate. So does my dad wherever he may be. My dad worked very hard for me and my sister, earning a savings for us from when I was only six and my sister was four. I do know that some of the money was from drugs and some other crimes, but that is not the point.

Still holding my hand, my dad told me that my grand-dad (Don's dad), whom I only remember seeing once, died in a car accident. He was wealthy and had also saved a lot for his three sons from an early age. In his will, he left half of the cash in his bank accounts to Grandma, his wife, and the remainder, including the family home, to the three sons. In good faith, he left Grandma, then a loving wife I guess, to look after both the money and the property till the boys were old enough to look after themselves. Grandma immediately bought a sports car and began making up for what she may have missed in her early twenties.

Soon, there were people, including estate agents, coming round to see the house. Grandma told the boys that the people were contractors whom she had invited to assess areas that required renovation, as she wanted to use the house as collateral for a loan. She was actually selling the house. She squandered her own share of the money and even blew the boys' shares. She sold the family home and disappeared to Hawaii with some Latino muchachito.

She asked her good neighbour and close friend to keep an eye on the boys while she went to Hawaii for a week-long break. With all house effects still in the house, no one suspected anything. No one knew about her plans till a postcard said she was sorry to have left her boys. She had found a new love and was making a new life in the sun in Hawaii. She said that she could not bear the thought of living in the same house with Granddad gone, that seeing her three boys would always remind her of him.

She later phoned her friend advising her to sell all the stuff in the garage and part of the furniture in the house to meet the bills and whatever my dad and his brothers would need on a daily basis. Everyone was gob smacked.

But the shocker was yet to come. Two weeks later my father and his two young brothers were visited by some strange, but kind, family, and asked when they would be moving out as they had bought the house. With the ground suddenly taken away from beneath their feet, you can imagine the confusion and anger the boys felt.

At fourteen—and my dad was wiser than I was at that age—Dad searched for a bank statement and went to try to acquire money from Granddad's account. Of course, he did not know the processes. The staff took him to meet the bank manager to whom my dad explained of Granddad's death a year earlier and the boys' current plight. It is then that he was told that Grandma had transferred all the money into some foreign account.

That day marked the descent of my dad and his brothers into poverty and the underworld. That also spelt the descent of Taxina into care twenty years later down the line. Twenty-four years later, the after-effects of that betrayal sent my dad into prison. Yes, in his early teens, my dad was short-changed by his own mother.

Ten years on, my dad learned his lessons quickly or should have. Full of love for his then-innocent wife, he also started savings for me and my little sister. He foolishly allowed my mum to be a signatory of our account, saying that since he was always up and about, and Mum was mostly at home, she should be able to meet any of our instant financial needs as we grew up. He asked Mum to always phone him about any money she would be withdrawing from our account and whatever she wanted to buy for us.

But each time Mum withdrew some money, by the end of that month, Dad always deposited twice the amount into the account. Mum discovered that and started creating all sorts of excuses for needing money, like school trips, musical equipment, and art materials for us girls. But in reality she, with her girlfriends, was blowing the money on beer and drugs.

My dad loathed drugs and never ever wanted any of his family to take them as he had seen too many lives wasted that way. So anyone can understand, I guess, his anger when he discovered that his very wife had been secretly taking drugs and wasting family savings on those drugs.

One day, my dad calmly asked Mum about the money and the drugs. Instead of apologizing and being mortified, she started swearing at him and stormed out of the house. She even went and shopped him to police about some crimes she knew about, and Dad went in. That broke Dad's heart and it broke mine even though I was only ten.

"Where is the love, Mummy?" I often say to her in my thoughts. "Grassing your man, shopping the very man you said was your soul mate all these years? The father of your two little princesses as you and him lovingly called us? Normally I would have looked up to you for a model of a woman. But what terribly evil creatures we women are. You turned your loving charm into prison term for him, and you smirked your lips to some poor new love, who probably is unknowingly awaiting his fate."

How can my dad ever trust another woman in his life? Fortunately or not, he only has girls, as he would have been at pains to find a positive message to tell his son about women.

Maybe this is why I am more friendly to boys than I am to women and girls, except for one girl called Barbit. I shall never understand these silly women. "Call your Mum silly?" I hear you protesting. Well, I cannot describe her any other better way. Only she knows what she missed while still with my dad.

"Love you, honey. Look after the princesses, darling; lots of love," were the words I remember hearing from my dad to his beloved, my mother, every morning and every evening. He would plant a loving kiss on her lips each day before leaving to work, or before taking us to school if it was his day. He even praised her for cooking, which my sister and I would be screaming was rubbish. "When you behave like that," was his routine statement when upset, "it upsets me!"

Too many times could I sense his anger and disappointment, but he always avoided mudslinging, not in our presence. Only once do I remember hearing him shout angrily at Mum, but that was in their bedroom. I only heard it because I was wide awake, reading some Mills and Boon. He may have had his failings, but he is the best dad, and I think he was an angel at home.

Of course Mum can now testify to Dad being an angel, as evidenced by the scar left by a split lip she suffered at the hands of her new man. He is her third and latest buttering ram, needle-pusher, gonzo of a boyfriend. Not even a slap did she ever get from my dad in the more than twelve years she was with him. And she grassed him. Shopped him to the coppers!

I can never imagine myself being so callous. I would love to lavish (and not destroy) my husband or children with money. Well, Reverend, now you do understand when I say that I do not have anyone to call a model of a woman, not even in my mum?

Hence, my questions are all justified. Do please think about them and give me some realistic answers. Even in care, I have more questions than answers.

Taxie XXX

CHAPTER 6

Could You Be My Brave New Model?

Candle Mews,
Radnor-cliff crescent
Folkestone,
CT20 2JQ

Today's date

Dear Prospective Carer,

Of all the possible jobs, if this one that tickled your fancy, you are coming in the right direction. Will you soon be fostering?

Then this secret is waiting for you. It is our secret, we, the children in care ("CHICs" as we fondly call ourselves) and Looked After Children, or LACs as the authorities prefer to call us.

As background information, we have an old testament, and a new testament that has yet to take roots. Welcome to this noble calling, for it is nothing less than that. Looking after young, impressionable, potential prime ministers, doctors, pilots, beauty queens, future celebrities, professors, fathers and mothers—cute little people like me simply has to be the noblest calling in life. But I still have not told you the secret yet.

In the Old Testament, under which we currently operate, our homes are always short staffed. Our managers have heavy workloads and meeting schedules. While seasoned but overworked staff leave jobs at a rate of one staff member every three months, new ones find overloaded managers and a system that pays peanuts and lacks the right training. These managers have little time and patience for the former.

For the New Testament, which starts operating with the next staff recruitment, we children are part of the boardroom. We have negotiated and pleaded with local authorities and staff to give each of us looked after children a choice in placement. We've asked that they support us with emotionally warm and homey company that is not suffocated by paperwork or fear of wrongdoing. Once they give us these, we shall blossom to the sky.

Authorities now know that a child in care is not just looking for a bed. Many of us did have a bed and roof where we came from. So we need more in any home, be it foster or residential. We need to be given an informed choice in selecting a new placement—not a blind date. In all fairness, we should be allowed to meet several prospective foster carers and choose the ones with whom we feel more at ease.

I know that some of the children in care are nightmares who cause hell to foster families. Shouldn't the prospective carers meet several of us, and learn our full history, so that they can, fully and knowingly choose whom to let into their families?

I hear someone saying, "What about those who are not chosen?"

Well, just as in football, I guess life has losers and winners. As my dad would say, "Every one becomes a winner at their time."

If one gave the wrong impression, or their history scared a prospective family, maybe they can be kept in a children's home for a year or two. Then they can be helped to re-learn how to live with others, with full knowledge of the consequences of not conforming. They can polish their behaviours, outgrow their poor actions, until they are accepted.

After all, carers still need to let us learn that the world out there gives you nothing for nothing. Even criminals use some form of self discipline and responsibility to survive. I know this as some of my friends are ex-cons from whom I learned a lot about life.

Moreover, what's the point of putting a 12 to 17 year old into foster care, when they are already, and possibly wrongly, opinionated from their biological parents? They are bound to create resistance and possibly attract abuse-bordering anger from carers unable to deal with open defiance.

Do you know what you mean to us, and what we wish you really were to us? Do you know what kind of a carer and or foster parent we would make, combining the best traits from each one of you?

We acknowledge that, like the children, carers come in a variety of personalities, cultures, and even influences. Oscar Wilde's words also apply to carers we met in this Old Testament: Some cause happiness wherever they go, and indeed others whenever they go. Having settled on the foster home, or residential home as the case may be, here below are the specifications for a prospective children's home carer.

Children's residential care is about children who believe they know what they want, even when it is the wrong thing. They have had it rough before, and they are edgy. The system calls them "challenging young people." These residents then make up a vulnerable and disadvantaged minority: some dogged by instances of child abuse and past broken down placements. But in reality, we are sweet, adorable, energetic, and passionate kids, waiting to be discovered, loved, and understood.

Imagine that we LACs were given the power to decide how our home should be run. Now that we are prepared for the boardroom, this is what we would say: We as residents need all around care and involvement in all plans and decisions. Once we are involved, we shall understand what goes on. We shall subsequently know how to communicate, and there shall be little to protest.

If we are helped to make a homely environment where we can happily play and the adult staff do not have a constant fear of making mistakes or losing their jobs, we shall not be likely to be out of education. We won't be starving for hugs, and none shall be so emotionally insecure as to risk teenage pregnancy. Well-fed and watered, and given hugs, even petty criminal activities would not be attractive.

Such is our dream for long-term, well-researched placement. Such is the new residential home where we can grow in a snug "homely" environment, with more opportunities to enjoy ourselves, and staff who are happy to be looked at as our "buddy" parents.

So should you fit the role as our home manager, you need to know how to plan and focus on our whole development. You will know how I thrive and fit in with groups of other children and in group dynamics that promote therapy and education through realistic but creative activities in both work and play.

I remember one of my super teachers, a teacher I still hate to have left. He made sure to take one child each day as his buddy in everything he did that day, except going to the toilet. He acted so genuinely that every child looked forward to his or her day. Fortunately, this teacher had his own matrix for selecting the child for the day, which I still have not understood. Whatever it was, he used it so well that you never predicted that the coming day would be yours.

So he kept us so positively excited that we went to all lengths to please him. Mind you, he never let you mess about, but he also took his time to discuss with you almost everything you cared to talk about. He would come down to your level to talk about the things that you indicated mattered to you.

I remember when it was my turn to be his right-hand person. He asked me what music I liked. I told him that I adored Craig David. He chatted away about not having known so much about Craig David, and asked me to sing to him at least one piece that I remembered. I sang him "The Rise and Fall." Mr. Size, as that was his name, was thrilled.

Three months later, when I had forgotten about it, he surprised me with posters of Craig David, showing his six-pack abdominal muscles. He had bought the posters especially for me, topped with two CDs, *7days* and *Born to do it*. To me, it was all hot stuff!

But it wasn't just me. A month earlier, I remember he bought a little math book with a calculator, and groovy pen that played music when you flicked the cover. The back of the book had a built-in small tape that played all the multiplication tables. He gave it to one boy he would be walking with that day. The boy had forgotten that he had told Mr. Size that he wanted to be a math wizard and teach math when he grew up. The boy was over the moon, and thoroughly surprised.

We were all green with envy. I remember wondering what he had seen in him, and why it wasn't me.

Another girl had said that she loved riding her bicycle but could not bring it to school for fear it would get nicked. Six months later, the girl was surprised with a strong security chain lock for her bike. We all went "Aah!" We knew better than to utter favouritism.

Mr. Size made every child feel important. He was as pleasant as he was strict. He never tolerated any fighting, playing in class, or flirting for those that were a little older. He did not hesitate to tell your parents if you played fools or ignored his warnings. I know there are rubbish parents that side with their children when their children behave poorly and challenge teachers. Yet I do not remember any parents that challenged Mr. Size. He was a teacher that we all cried to leave.

With such strong abilities with children, if Mr. Size were a children's residential staff member, none of his children would at all be involved with the police. He could tell a troubled child from miles away. He created emotional support in scenarios that eliminated any non-illness related absences from school.

Although, a mere teacher, Mr. Size took all matters into his own hands and rarely sent you to Mr. Winker, the headmaster's office. In "care speak," he was not "manager dependent." No. Mr. Size was not. I can only judge him from what he taught me, but I believe every child he taught went away with a positive feeling that affirmed his or her self-confidence.

The right-hand child of the day did everything *with* the teacher and not *for* the teacher, mind you. Mr. Size treated every activity as a valuable, educational opportunity, even if it meant cooking blood pudding on a picnic or cleaning the toilets and washing the windows.

He consciously involved you in discussions regarding topics that ranged from how the school could be improved to how you were doing in school and your dream job for the future. Most importantly, he always asked us what more we, each of us, would like to know about our individual ambitions.

While a few of us claimed not to have innate sporting abilities, Mr. Size made everyone, boys and girls, try everything: football, volleyball, netball, basketball, and lawn tennis. Then, he asked us to choose what we liked and told us to stick to it. No wonder our school had one of the best teams in everything!

Thinking back, everything he did was some kind of therapeutic and an educational process that was made into so much fun that we looked forward to doing more the following day. Mr. Size made sure that most of the people in class were friends. He made groups that worked together on a project for three weeks and rearranged us so that everyone learned to work well with everyone else.

This was a rarity in an inner London school where politicians and high-strung parents are too happy to throw spanners in the works for anyone who braves to make a decent teacher.

Yes, just as paperwork kills patients (as reported by my friend Sarah writing to me from Arundel mental hospital unit), in care procedures ruin children's futures. If procedures kill children's futures, inadequately trained staff and social workers who cannot be social, make their coffins.

Are you up for a positive challenge? Are you confident in your own skills and authority? Able to participate in decision-making for individual children alongside social workers and teachers? Are you able to not be manager-dependent? Would you be ready to help turn bored children's lives around and, wherever possible, help them to have good experiences and new opportunities?

Below are some attributes we seriously would want you to have. You shall need to:

- Help us—much as we may not initially like it—to create frequent contact between us and our biological families, such as having joint dinners and sports days.
- Be able to use natural judgment, unlike in the Old Testament, to give children selflessly loving hugs that promote trust, self-esteem, and emotional well-being.
- Be ready to accept that children need to be exposed to some risk for them to learn how to manage it.
- Have the zeal to make long-term, water-tight plans that have instant back up to save us from the current culture, which makes children endure too many placements and lose irreplaceable schooling and childhood fun through frequent and sudden moves.
- Accept that, while sometimes annoying to adults, some messing about is natural for children along their path of growth.
- Be strong enough to draw a firm but loving line of authority when boundaries are pushed too much.
- Be alert and intuitive enough to sense learning difficulties that may be disguised as behaviours.
- Be loving enough of children to want to have your own, as a guarantee of your understanding of our demands for safety, emotional security, and holistic development.
- Be willing to take ongoing responsibility for a child's development beyond your shift and even working tenure.
- Be willing to listen, guide, and even sometimes defend our positions if the imminent institution decision will be damaging to us in the long term (such as frequent and sudden moves).

- Be imaginative enough to fill our lives with responsible excitement to detract us from the false thrills of such habits as smoking.
- Be willing to gather evidence and challenge the status quo, to demonstrate and demand that children in care should categorically be supported into their twenties. Children from stable homes, growing with the support of constant friends, living in a family environment with an ongoing social cultural climate are supported into university and still fail out there and return to the warmth of the home. (How would any one expect any different from us, who often have disturbed or delayed development and often lack established social structures to fall back on?)
- Be willing to make the job your own and grow with it, while making a homely house of your residence.
- Have the personality to foster an environment that enables properly trained staff to analyse and adequately respond to the variety of needs that make us flourish as whole individuals.
- Be knowledgeable enough to ensure that the development plan for each child covers not just food and education, but complete health care as well.
- Have the zeal to call for the £500 education support provided by the local authority for additional tuition or resources for each of us children at the earliest sign of need.
- Be able to appreciate that "too many cooks spoil the broth." The fewer the staff nurturing each child, the more responsible and focused the services become and, consequently, the easier it is for each child to venture to trust someone.
- Be willing to push for an establishment or mending of relations, even if guarded, between us and our biological parents. While the current testament insinuates that failed parents are evil, the reality is that most became what they were by surrounding forces and a political society that ignored their plight. Maybe they did not know how to cry for help or their cries fell on deaf ears. Or perhaps they suffered from economic pressures from which no one helped them correctly.

My parents may be bad—I have a big axe to grind with my mum! But they are my parents nonetheless. Much as I adore Angella, one of my long-gone carers, I would not replace my parents. I would like us to mend fences. If social services had been willing to help me grow up all around, they also would have helped my parents be more responsible. They would have talked to them to find out areas in which they need help and could have shown them what else they could improve on and guide them on where to get help.

I want all parents to be accountable and responsible for their children. They should be given space if they need it to re-grow, or to give children a breathing chance. But do not replace the parents. Ultimately, foster and residential homes should at best be like boarding schools, from which children should be able to later leave and re-link with their parents and move on. They should be able to use the additional one-to-one tuition grant to enable every child to leave care equipped to earn a respectable leaving.

That is currently not what is happening. As Rob Williams, writing for the *Independent*, once said: Of the 60,000 looked-after children in care, nearly three-quarters will leave care with no formal qualifications and only one percent will ever go on to enter any kind of university education. One-fifth of looked-after children are homeless two years after leaving care and one-quarter of the people in prison were once in care.

I guess this is official and justifiably worrying as this bloke, Rob Williams, was the Deputy Children's Commissioner for England from 2006 to 2008. You bet the man knows what he is talking about in the *Independent*!

This is unlike out in the continent where 95 percent of children go on to vocational education and are so emotionally secure that there is minimal crime and teen pregnancy rates. I also learned that based on education and otherwise indecisive meetings about our welfare, you, the social workers, our main welfare advocates, are the most junior persons in the room. Rotten raspberries! How can I trust you to successfully lobby my cause?. As my new carer, please be better than that. The specifications above are your recipe for success.

This is one of the rarest of the secrets I had promised you, my readers. Now that you know what it would take to make me a success, will you please be my brave new model? Once more welcome to our house, you beloved carers and all loving parents. Do bring your love and warm hugs with you as we move on to the next secret.

Lots of love,

Taxie XXX

CHAPTER 7

We Fear Turning Seventeen

Candle Mews,
Radnor-cliff crescent
Folkestone,
CT20 2JQ

Today's date

Dear Narjis,

Do they say: "One for Sorrow and Two for Joy"? Today, I have been thinking about you. Did someone ever tell you that the week you went away on leave Candle Mews looked and felt different? The same rules that we follow every day suddenly seemed hard to follow. The usual cooked breakfast we have on Saturdays tasted different. Sausages, eggs, bacon, toast, and baked beans—all did not taste edible. This is not flattery, Narjis. But you did seem to have taken some social spirit with you. We may not have said it before, but that is how much we love and miss you, Narjis.

Maybe just as getting ill reminds one of mortality, but your absence reminded me of the dreaded "seventeenth" birthday. Although no one will quote it to us in writing, most of us children in care do realise that turning seventeen is a "make or break" birthday. It is the birthday that other children enjoy as the last one before adulthood. For many of us, it is a birthday we dread as it points to the exit door. Out of the house, out of the home, and maybe out of contact with Narjis. I dread that birthday.

You see, most of us have never had a lasting family to grow in, learn, and practice living. Every day we have hints that we may soon be on our own, to swim or sink, brave the world or die. We hear of stories of the many unlucky ones who are introduced to the so-called pathways, ways that must be fast-track schooling about managing life, huge as it is.

Narjis, this is where you make a difference as you pour love into every statement you make when teaching me to make those pancakes and fajitas. As you know, the case conference did not go my way at school. Despite my home tutor trying to help me so much, if I get moved from Candle Mews before my GCSEs, I shall be another sorry story. The usual dismal litany: missed schooling, wasted GCSEs opportunities, and bleak career prospects.

What do I have to look forward to? I shall have no career and no real family ties to whom I can cry out. If only someone could link me to my dad and point me to some alternatives? What life is scrambling for a pittance, jobbing in the sweltering kitchen of a McDonald's or some canteen, scrubbing dishes and wishing longingly for an end? Now I fear that this life may be my lot when I turn seventeen.

Seventeen is the year when every looked after child is considered "weaned," when the children's home and/or foster parents are no longer bound to keep that child.

Yet this applies strictly only to looked after children. Or do you, Narjis, know any family that believes that their child is mature enough to be independent at such an age? How many of them are really budgeting masters, when even adults struggle with their finances? I have good dreams, dreams of freedom and financial independence, dreams of wearing a serene smile like your smile, Narjis. But only if I can cross age seventeen with a definitely outward folding plan of the future.

I know you have a life, Narjis, but promise me that you shall not leave Candle Mews before I do. For when I turn seventeen—or whenever I may be told to leave Candle Mews to go God knows where—I shall need your comforting words. I shall need to know where I can reach you, even if by snail mail. It is not exactly like you belong to me, Narjis, but do believe me, I carry you in my heart and treasure having known you. It is not long from now, hardly two years, before I will walk the longest mile a girl has to walk in life, a mile that only gets lighter when I think of your smile beside me.

Lots of Love,

Taxie XX

CHAPTER 8

Calling Sonya, Social Worker

Candle Mews,
Radnor-cliff crescent
Folkestone,
CT20 2JQ

Today's date

Dear Sonya,

This letter is long overdue and has been drafted for months now. It is a letter I have been writing in my mind beginning a week after you were introduced into my life as my social worker. Sonya, I admired your very white and well-set teeth. They give you such a gorgeous smile. I do wish you could use that smile a bit more often, but that is a subject of another letter. You have always wondered what goes on in my little mind, as I have mostly kept myself to myself. Today, I decided to let you in. Brace yourself for this emotionally packed ride into my inner life.

Besides my tutor, you are probably the most influential person in the current part of my life. I do not know if you already know this, but I do love you Sonya. You gave me a chance to experience a different life, away from the confusion in my own home, and I honestly thank you.

On the other hand, you sometimes present me a very confusing picture. At these times, you are the person I love to hate and the person I would love to love, if you gave me a chance. You know who and what you represent, but I certainly do not know who you represent. You definitely do not and would not realistically represent me, not with your current view and attitude.

While I am a tormented and angry young person, or so you and my carers have said, I hate what you neglect to do and, sometimes, what you actually do and represent in your official capacity. But this has nothing to do with who you are in your private life. Trust me. I would never hurt a fly.

In this letter, I shall give you a piece of my mind, what I feel over what I am going through and have gone through. The letter tells you my thoughts about our relationship, what I think it is and what it should be, what I find your role in my life to currently be and what it should be on your case load. Are you prepared, Sonya, to look at your roles, for once from the perspective of a child you have assumed to be looking after?

You shall be perfectly justified to lose the plot as you read the letter, as I perfectly understand that you are used to power, authority, and even influence. I fully know that you can change my placement, my happiness, or even the course of my life with just a drop of ink on paper. However, if you pay a bit more attention today, give me just one ear, your attitude towards us children in care may never be the same. What is more is that you could possibly enjoy your job even more.

I really wish you had the chance to correct the preconceptions or misconceptions, which I am bound to have. But my view represents life seen from this side of the fence. Currently, our relationship is that of master and puppet. At times, you pose like the police, and I am the accused being represented by you. While I could choose my advisor if I had to, I did not choose you. Maybe I could have asked some questions or given you a trial period before making you my long-term representative.

If you ask me, our relationship should have been one where only shared, clarified targets of growth and partnership mattered, and not power and age. You should have been my experienced partner, and I should have been the pliant yet alert associate, willing to learn. I should have been able to tell you my hopes and fears. But currently, unless you adjust your approach after reading this letter, I am afraid that you shall have to keep guessing or rely on my teacher and friends, who probably can give you only annotated versions of who I am.

At Blue Lodge, I met Thomas, you were his social worker also, and he had his own version. We find you're playing the police towards our parents, regardless of the conditions, and then trying to play the advocate to children's homes, foster carers, and schools. This is a confusing and contradictory role. Is this your own hypocrisy or do you get conflicting and impossible roles from your bosses?

Sonya, I know that you probably mean good to us, every single day you wake up to go to work. However, whether it is your own fault or not, we children in care feel looked after but not *cared* for. Yes, we are even called "Looked After Children," but we want more than just to be "looked after." I remember you saying that you have children, a boy and a girl. Do the children you are looking after receive the same treatment as your own biological children?

Currently, we are observed, made to do things, and guarded from doing wrong or causing trouble. It is an artificial life, guided by home managers, bound books, emails, and projected needs. Our advocates, whoever they may be, can only be those who understand us and, hence, those who have built a proper rapport with us.

For example, at Stone House, the first children's home I was placed in, there was Angela. Elderly as she may have been, certainly older than my Mum, she understood me. Angela did. She knew how and when to talk to me about things. She cared for and about me without making me feel favoured, quizzed, or picked on.

Having so opened herself to me and taken the time to understand how I felt, she came across as easy to talk to. I did not mind being corrected by Angela. In that sense, control had its clear place in my development. Just as I feared and respected Daddy, I would not dare to let Angela know that I smoked. I never ever wanted to disappoint her. In a way, without really trying, Angela set boundaries for me and did a job even better than my poor mum.

Sonya, your colleagues and you need to think of ways to give us a realistic care experience, one that makes us feel a part of the community. A care "plus" experience both you and I can remember with smiles should replace your expectancy of trouble and readiness to control difficult behaviour.

Many of us have been shunted from one placement to another, and we yearn for acceptance. We yearn for love. We yearn to love you all back, have a laugh, and when in the wrong, be told off, just like any child from a traditional loving home. That is why moving us between homes causes us untold heartaches, mental anguish and uncertainties about our own identities. For example, the message I received when I was moved was that no one wanted me and that no one loved me. Yes the moving says that we are born into the wide world with no one for us. Have you ever imagined the tragedy of having no one to relate to? Have you ever felt the pain of not belonging?

We would love to have someone to trust, but only if that person speaks a positive language for our positive development. From the last three failed placements, you can trust me to know how staff can use children in care to whip each other and even to satisfy their own curiosities and failures in their private lives.

Many of us have emotional emptiness that makes us offer ourselves to abuse in search of acceptance. For example, Dalia, one of the three girls at June Cottage, left the three years ago when she was sixteen. She went to live on her own in a council flat. Barely three months later, she wrote to me that she was pregnant but did not know the father of her child She named George, the driver who used to drive her to Bristol to see her mum, as the most likely father. However, Dalia said that George had raped her several times on the way to and from Bristol. But she added that she actually flirted with him, and wanted him to do it. It made her feel valued, even for a short time. She confided in me that she had also slept with Marten, the cook, the handy man at her previous home, and had been sexually abused several times by her granddad when she was twelve.

Even after leaving care, Dalia said that she quickly found a flat of her choice by sleeping with one of the men at the benefits office. Now she has three children in three years from three different men, none of whom is committed to live with her. She left two men with not just broken hearts but broken families as well. She regrets nothing and moves on looking for her next fool. Actually, one of her three children is from the husband of her next-door neighbour, with whom she has now fallen out.

With two children to look after and expecting a third, Dalia is already looking worn out and barely has time to rest. She is planning to get training for a career, but her focus at reading is not up to scratch. She says she eyes a dream job to train for, but three young children in three years are not going to leave her with much free time, are they?

She is already planning to give her first born, Leo, up for adoption or into care. Her own mum does not want anything to do with Dalia's "little puppies," as she calls them. She repeatedly tells her that after her own failure to raise Dalia, every woman should look after the children she bears or have none at all. Sonya, I am no exception to that thinking.

There is one maintenance guy who talks to me like I am a princess. He is never suggestive or anything, but he greets me and all the other children with natural love and makes us feel wanted and valued. None of the carers ever talk to us like that. We cannot help but warm up to such people. Going weak in the knees for such a man, though he is probably older than my dad, is only natural, I guess. Lately I try to avoid him and go to my room each time he comes into the house. Yet I keep my ear to the door, as hearing his voice alone makes my world brighter.

Matthew has always missed his late granddad who died three months before he was put into care. Matt still feels that he was the one person who understood him. He is thirteen and has been moved three times in the last three-four years. He now lives with foster parents. Like many, Matt doesn't feel that he belongs enough in the home. While in Corner House, from where he moved into foster care, he says that he had no real restraints on behaviour. Children learned to swear at each other and were not really praised for anything.

In the foster home, foster parents tried integrating him into their lives. However, having lived with ridicule and negative labelling, not used to encouragement, he remained suspicious of their motives. He misinterpreted all their acts of kindness and was not able to easily accept a compliment.

He deeply envied the daughter in the family for receiving warm hugs from the foster parents, and he felt left out. Apparently, he was still angry from the treatment he had been receiving at Corner House. He also resented his social worker, whom he felt had let him into that home. However, he vented his anger and frustrations at the wrong people.

Given a chance to go out and play after school, Matt teamed up with some local boys. In search of fun, they went into the churchyard and practiced martial arts, kicking at grave stones. The broke and moved a few and some passers-by informed the police. After being chased, of the six, only Matt and a younger boy were arrested; the others escaped.

Asked why he joined the boys in desecrating the graves, he replied that the other boys were good company and he did not have to prove anything to be accepted by them. Matt was not charged, but he received a lasting label as a potential criminal and senseless vandal. Even the "Meticulous Matt" lost his good reputation at a tender age. Such is the cost and price we children pay in exchange for acceptance and unconditional love.

As I grow up in my teen years, my need to talk to someone, to confide in someone, seems to grow and take a different form. I need people to try to understand me and to help me create my own identity. However, women carers in whom I can confide seem to be particularly mean and scathing of teen girls. They put me off. On the other hand, some male carers listen so well. In the process, their eyes say that they have never seen anyone as gorgeous and often they start flirting. I have slept with such a man, not because he coaxed me, but because he gave me the attention I needed. But I was soon moved to another house when the manager suspected what was going on.

You may not understand this if you have never suffered from emotional insecurity, but this is the damage that not being accepted, not being loved causes to children. The damage is actually lasting, but instead of being helped with parental love, we are judged and moved.

Sonya, you may wish to open your eyes and realise that we children in care still are abused even under the strictest office regulations. Our abuse comes in various forms from various members of staff and the public as we reach out to be heard and be loved.

It is like a child that burns his fingers while trying to pull a frying egg from the pan. But many of us suffer in silence. Even after the death of Victoria Climbie, social welfare and social workers still work in isolation, sometimes deliberately undermining one another or even defending each other against us. But who does a victimised child turn to when being uprooted to another placement is the government's favoured intervention?

Many of us choose to suffer in silence, hoping that we either outgrow it, or will move on someday, or the perpetrator will go away. This is what Bob Marley succinctly said:

> Man to man is so unjust,
> *We* children don't know who to trust.

Even clear hints of SOS are missed by some social workers. Maybe you need to visit us more often and stay a bit longer than the traditional two hours to learn how to read us? Currently, I guarantee you Sonya that, as my social worker, you know much less about me than the carers in the homes where I am placed.

I once heard from my manager that you have been taught how to communicate with children and adolescents. I also found it interesting that those in charge of more troublesome children are offered more training opportunities than those who look after meek ones. Do your lessons really include how to listen to us? If you cannot demonstrate by listening to more than my voice, if you cannot acknowledge the facts that are behind my perennial anger against the adult world, how do you expect trust from me?

The adult world piles its failures on us and overloads us, choking us off from growing. I know that some of us have had to pay with our lives for your failures. The pretty Victoria Climbie would turn in her grave to know that the inefficiencies that permitted her death have not gone away.

Is it so difficult to understand us or are you simply being too bookish to care for us? Is it because we are *just* children in care to you that you choose to be this mechanical to us? I do hope that your children tell rosy stories about you. Could you please invite me for a picnic with your kids on one of their birthdays?

Maybe, just as you study your own children and respond to their needs, you can coordinate among yourselves whenever you get reports, hints, or suspect that a child is in distress. Why is it difficult to gather the necessary information about the child's problem and personality circumstances, such as his or her own version and that of significant others, to help you react quickly?

The probable answer is that you are not close enough to us to understand our signals for distress. But if you did, maybe you could identify a more accommodating placement that blends nature, nurture, and emotional-scar-clearing love.

We children always hoped and believed that removing us from

abusive or harsh environments would place us in homes we would grow in and love. Having been born and lived in a family part of my life, I still want to believe that there are couples that miss children for the love and laughter we bring. You just have to find them, learn their routines, and match our placements.

Having a waiting list of foster parents could reduce the distress and bad habits we pick up in children's homes. Children's homes have been an emergency shelter for a child awaiting fostering, but many children stay there forever. I know one, Christopher, who went to June Cottage long before I came there. But I was moved on and he was left there. All he learns in that shelter is swearing, smoking, practicing killer moves from violent DVDs, and drinking.

I even heard on television that the average social worker has seventeen to twenty case loads, as opposed to the manageable number of twelve. Similarly, in most of these homes, managers care more about rotas and shift patterns that suit their private lives, than they do about what creates consistency and continuity for our development.

How do I know this? I hear staff complain. Has no child ever told you that when you complain about your jobs and staff relations, when you act bored on excursions with us, you create a yawning emotional vacuum in our lives?

Each time someone we have become used to changes their work pattern to suit their school children's times or other family circumstances, we are constantly reminded that we are second. It tells us that we can only share the emotional dregs of the love and tender care reserved for your own families. We are street children, who must survive on bread crumbs after normal children have had their fill.

To illustrate my point, let me tell you about Temporary Tim. I did warn you at the beginning of our journey that it would be emotionally challenging, yet enlightening. Tim has been in care from the age of eight. He has had six placements that have all broken down, and when he came to an adjoining flat at Corners House, they called him "Temporary Tim" because no one knew if he would stay this time.

He cannot speak properly, he is anxious of public places, and he needs assurance with even basic acts, such as using the toilet. Tim is ever so angry because he is never understood, and he feels that society is always changing the goal posts for him. On the other hand, society, through misunderstanding him, has labelled him "very challenging."

But how would you react if the people you spoke to did not understand you and never spoke your language? What support would you expect from someone who did not understand what you were saying? If you signed to them, and they responded with a bewildered look? What dream or quality of life, if any, would you expect if such was the type of carer or support worker you got in five out of seven days? That is what Temporary Tim has to live with. Is it any wonder that he is so frustrated? Is he correctly labelled as an "aggressive young man with challenging behaviours"?

Imagine yourself as the social worker for Tim, and try planning his care and life. Currently, Tim's social care is dictated by one or two carers who can play balls with him or take him for a walk once a week. He has five other carers who, each time they are meant to be supporting him, stay in the adjoining room. A lockable door separates the "staff room" from Tim's corridor, which leads to his lounge, toilet, bathroom, and bedroom. As soon as they have given him food or something to drink, they quickly return to their little room, shutting and locking the door behind them, petrified of Tim's "aggression."

Tim is in care in a children's home, but, Sonya, is Tim in "care" or in "prison"? I know that money is poured in for his care, and daily reports are written about his progress. How well these reflect Tim's social and personal progress, I do not know. As an authority, would you honestly tell me where Tim's life is going? Tim is on a weight control diet. To what end is such a diet when all he does is sleep on the couch, mostly getting up late with only breakfast and lunch to look forward to?

The one time that Tim joined us in the garden, planting flowers, he seemed to enjoy it so much that he did not want to stop and return to his flat. But he has since not been given another chance as the manager said that a risk assessment for Tim's participation in gardening had not been done.

Tim does not even have a make believe world, not a dream nor a planned day to cling to. Outings are very seldom, due to lack of or shortage of regular staff that know and understand his needs and communication abilities. Yet one wonders how expensive it can be to train dedicated carers in Makaton or British sign language, when such people could provide appropriate daily care for Tim? Could that not give him a better quality of life? Now one of the two staff that understood Tim has left for a new job. Tim has completely withdrawn from most interactions, and the managers are now calling for a psychiatrist to reassess him.

Such is the scandalous impact of staff turnover on children in care. Just when Tim was beginning to open up to one member he thought he could trust, that member leaves, and Temporary Tim must start afresh with someone as good as a stranger. Is it any surprise to you that after several failed placements or changes in key workers, we harden up?

To some of us, it becomes a repeat of the abandonment we suffered earlier. It becomes a constant trigger of the yearning for our family homes in spite of that life having been far from perfect. Oh, if only Social Services solved my problems in my own home, if only they helped my parents to cope with their challenges, without having to move us children out. We still yearn for some, even imaginary, emotional security we may have had in these rocky teen years.

You may want to remember that we are so far removed from society that the lasting picture of society is the one we make from seeing our carers and the television. Besides our parents, the way our carers treat us could unconsciously set precedence on how we may treat our children or someone in our care later.

I, for one, think that you deliberately take a make believe role, pretending to be substitute parents. But you play that role badly. Uncomfortable as it may be, could you please remind us what we can realistically expect from you as social workers? And of course, what you expect from us, more than just the dos and don'ts, as we reach various phases of our lives. Learn from me, the insider.

Remember what I said about Angella from Stone House? One could not help but open up to her. She always invited me to join her in her activities around the house: cooking, scrubbing the lounge, dusting and cleaning windows. In that process, Angella taught me the joy of being prepared and organised in life. I now can happily make my bed on waking up, without waiting for prompts from anyone.

At Stone House, I had a friend, Jennie, who was kicked by her key worker and sexually abused by the handyman, but she was too scared to tell anyone. Of course, Jennie told me later that she feared that no one would believe her, and Laura, her key worker, always threatened her. So she lived in fear of her key worker, the very person who should have been her rock. I easily could have told Angella if anything like that ever had happened to me.

Unfortunately, Angella left, and immediately thereafter, I was moved to Juniper Lodge where I became just another number.

Anyway, Sonya, the point is that care workers need to be accessible, have interest beyond mere duty, and we shall reciprocate. We may seem to be pushing boundaries repeatedly, but over time, three-quarters of us respond positively. You may want to remember that the way you treat us, and our responses to you, form the building blocks of our view of the world beyond the door.

While we plead for acceptance, we do not cry for sympathy. Yes people may have used me to get their ends, emotionally or otherwise. I may only be another tool in the handyman's box, but I keep my eyes open, not just for fun, but for love and cues to making a real independent life. I may have appeared defensive, but I am still looking for acceptance and love. From seeing Angella, I now believe in love, and I believe that there is still some goodness in the society.

Nevertheless, I do not want any more of the inhumane treatment mated out to the likes of Temporary Tim who cannot even speak for himself. If only all carers cared and all social workers were social, Sonya, I would never have written this letter to you.

By any means, Sonya, you are welcome to give me your reactions. Do let me know when you want to come and talk. I shall make you a strong cup of lemon tea, which I understand you love. I shall then play Bob Marley for you from my Nokia phone, and like buddies, we shall share one headphone each. If I hurt you in this letter, I shall wholeheartedly say that I am sorry and tell you "No Woman, No Cry". Thereafter maybe together we shall jam on to "One Love."

Taxie XXX

CHAPTER 9

How I found love in tears

Candle Mews,
Radnor-cliff crescent
Folkestone,
CT20 2JQ

Today's date

Dear Sara,

This letter is to you. I know you do not know me because we have never met, but last Wednesday my friends and I went to a movie to watch *Kung Fu Panda*. It was one of the most hilarious and entertaining movies I have ever watched. It made my day. More than that, Sara, I sat next to a girl with whom I immediately clicked.

We became good friends and talked at length after the movie. We went and had pizza together and shared a few heart-to-heart secrets. She told me about her big sister whom she loves very much. She showed me her picture and she was amazingly beauty. Sadly, her big sister is in a mental hospital for self harm, depression, believing that there is no meaning to life, and attempted suicide.

My new friend's name is Victoria and she prefers to be called Vicky. You can guess her sister's name. Yes, it is Sara. You.

Vicky told me that you enjoy receiving and reading letters. Since I cannot send you an email, I suggested we become pen friends. I shall write you as many letters as I can about my life in care. You too can write me about your life in the hospital and what you do the rest of the week. Tell me about the loving people you meet and what progress you are making. You know, Sara, the best time to write letters is in the evening just before going to bed. I write letters, and then fill my diary, and finally, I have learned to say a little prayer to God, whatever and wherever he is.

In this first letter, Sara, I shall let you into the private part of my life and my heart. Not even my mum or my boyfriend knows the story I am about to tell you. So Sara count yourself very trusted to be told this very private story.

My good friend Vicky told me in confidence that you are disturbed, that you find no meaning in life at all, that except for your baby brother, who is only one year old, you think no one loves you—not your mum, not your sister, and definitely not your stepdad. She says that you complain of stomach aches, headaches, that you experience sadness, emptiness, despair, loss of appetite, sleep problems, and loss of interest in nearly everything. Trust me to know what that is. I learned it from my mother. Those are clear signs of being depressed.

However, your mistrust of everyone does not give Vicky a chance. She says she has so much love for you and cares so much that she misses you every day. She told me that since you and your boyfriend went separate ways, you have lost all interest in everything in life.

Your sister has shown me your picture. Sarah, you have such amazing beauty. Your olive, silky skin so tender, your teeth whiter than rice, and your breath like a summer breeze. Better than Marilyn Monroe, you could truly have your choice of men, if you did not let the one frog fool your mind with unkind words. Those are just words, which if you only push out of your mind, you will find true joy and the prince of your heart. You have green sparkling eyes.

At eighteen, you do not have the acne blemishes that torment many of us teenagers. I hear that your ever flowing golden hair is natural, requiring minimal attention. I understand you have such a gentle but musical voice that can only be compared to that of Leona Lewis.

I cannot believe that with your beauty, you have let yourself be sunk so low by some undeserving little man. Maybe you did not look at him right. He was not a man, but just a silly, immature boy. Yes he was just a boy, yes even Beyonce could have done a better job at being a boy, don't you think?

Your sister does not understand you at all. She wishes she did, but feels she has tried very hard to get through to you. Since you are pining for love, since it is love that hang you out to dry, let's talk about love. We shall talk about the starry nights, the moonlit nights, the darkest nights, and the nights of discovery.

Sara, in life and in love, we lose and learn, and we make the best of the moment. Enjoy the sunset as it turns the sky a crimson blue, as change blows a wind of love, a new promise for you. Let go of men. They have their place, but they do not pretend to be our heroes. If we let them, trust me Sara, we shall sacrifice our whole lives to them.

That was the cause of the death of Marilyn Monroe, that immortal icon of beauty. At that moment you want even the lousiest mother to cuddle you. So try and mend bridges with your mother.

Men leave us crying and wringing our hands and they leave. They tour the world, enjoy themselves, making more fools of other new gullible girls. I learned it all from my mother. Love the men, but do not sell them your soul. Keep your soul as it is the sure thing that keeps your feet on the ground.

You can even smile and call their bluff, even if they try to shout aloud that you are ugly. Sour grapes, is all they say. As my dad used to say, a failed nun has no good word about any convent. Any bad words anyone says do not necessarily make us so, unless we agree to consider ourselves that way. That is the biggest lesson that I smack myself for when I catch myself crying from someone else's comment about me.

Yes Sara, I have been there, even though I am younger than you. I have travelled that road and have accompanied adults walking the road. Having kept my eyes wide open, I probably saw more and learned more from experiences than others whose eyes were blurred with tears. I do not have to wait and make the same blunders to learn. Remember the song of hope?

> *Soft as the voice of an angel, breathing a lesson unheard;*
> *Hope with a gentle persuasion whispers her comforting word*
> *Wait till the darkness is over, wait till the tempest is gone*
> *Hope for the sunshine tomorrow, after the shower is gone*
> *Whispering hope, oh how welcome thy voice*
> *Making my heart in its sorrow rejoice*
> *Whispering hope, oh how welcome thy voice*
> *Making my heart in its sorrow rejoice.*

It still rings true. Write the song in your heart. Sara, the song truly was written for you and me.

Yes, you almost killed yourself, thinking you almost had everything until your boyfriend changed his mind. But who tells you that he holds the key to your life? Have you not heard that "almost" doesn't count? Tell yourself that you are free, for you are. Say you hold your life, for you do.

There is nothing you lost as every lesson has a cost.

How did Judas miss heaven? Being a loner, he missed out learning from the other eleven. So you may learn from me as I learned from my mother. I know I shall make a better lover and a better mother than her. Sara, if you want a reminder, then say my name to yourself. Reread my letters and you shall feel stronger.

Here, let me tell you my story. It is a story of loss and discovery, of pain and gain, of shame and prospective fame, as my love enjoys saying my name. This is a story of how I found lasting love in the rubble of shame.

For about a year and half, I used to go around with this group of boys almost every single day. They all lived in Tooting. Everyone said that they were not "boys" but "men," but to me, they were not men. They were just boys. The oldest was about 24, then 23, 19, and the youngest was 18.

You see, I hate hanging about with people my age because they are nothing but trouble, they are not mature enough, and they get on my nerves. Except for the likes of Vicky, with whom I clicked immediately, most of my friends are older people, and I get on with them a lot better. Also I hate hanging around with girls because they are too bitchy. They like hurting each other's feelings.

Prepare yourself for a surprise Sara. Most of my mates are boys, but I am straight. Besides Vicky, your sister whom I have just met recently, I have Julia as my bosom friend. She knows me like the back of her hand. By the way, my little sister is also called Vicky. Daddy called her Vicky, and mummy called her Amy. She prefers to be called Vicky, though mum insinsists on calling her Amy. I call her both interchangeably, and she does not really mind.

Being straight is the source of this story. I have known the heartaches of the teen times. I have known the heart breaks of creating one's identity. Yes Sara, I know the cost of dreaming dreams that no two people exactly share. These are dreams that end in tears. But my tears watered a seed of love, and now listen to this.

It was a dark cold October night. It was the coldest night of that month. Everything seemed dead cold, even though snow had not started. Outside, there was absolutely no one to be seen on the street. The trees were silent, so still they stood as if uttering one breath could make them someone's dinner. It was as if everyone was hiding from something, too scared to walk out of their front doors.

Yet somehow, I had felt very bored at home. I thought, "Taxina, take a walk although it is cold. Say hi to the boys. There always is bound to be someone at the club or at least around the local KFC." So I walked out. When I was at the top of my road, I could see the whole road going downhill. The lights bent up and down with the road all the way to the bottom. Everything felt rather eerie, much like the premonition one feels in a horror movie. It was as if I was part of a scene with all the houses, trees, road lights, foxes, and all.

I had decided to meet some of my mates, Davis and Noel, halfway, as they would be coming round to my house at this time. My mum wanted to meet them. Here I was waiting for them. Unfortunately, Dominic was not coming as he was busy with God-knows-what at that time of the evening. Actually, I was glad he did not end up coming, as you shall soon know why.

Soon, before the two arrived, I started feeling hot under the collar. Beads of sweat were forming on my forehead, despite the weather being cold. My stomach felt as if I would get sick. This was a normal group of bad vibes for me. I felt nervous. I no longer looked forward to meeting the boys. Such was the feeling that preceded a serious family fight, especially my mum fighting with her partner. Such a fight would not end till late the next day. My sister and I would be up all night with my dog hiding under the bed.

Whenever I felt vibes like that, something negative happens. I am not so sure if that is the way things are meant to happen, or if I have learned to anticipate the negatives so much that I bring them on. The latter is more likely, as you shall soon see.

When Davis and Noel arrived, they would not talk to me. I extended my fist for the usual power greeting, but they just walked past, going to my house. I followed them in as they knocked.

You see Mum's is an average semi-detached, terraced house. As soon as you enter, you are on the landing, which for us is always littered with shoes. To your left are stairs leading up to two bedrooms and a bathroom. One of those rooms was mine, shared with my little sister, while the other was rented out to Joleen, who later became my friend. To your right, is a lounge that leads on to the kitchen and another outside door. Directly opposite the front door is a third bedroom, which was the one my mum used.

So on arrival, I quickly went up to my room to hang my coat and use the loo before joining the boys and everybody downstairs. Back in the lounge, I also found Julia. She had arrived as soon as I left, and I could not see her as I went up. As soon as I entered the lounge I happily introduced the boys to my mum, my mum's partner, and Joleen my mum's friend who lived with us. Julia was my next-door neighbour and my close friend whom the boys already knew. The boys also already knew my little sister.

It turned out that my mum just wanted to chat with the boys whom I had talked about. They chatted at length, talked to everyone else, but they would not talk to me. I was being left out and it felt horrible. I also felt horrible and empty inside.

You see Davis and I are still best mates. I also got along with Noel. He was a good friend, but not as close as Davis. Every time I tried to speak to them, they would pretend not to have heard me. Davis' birthday was just ten days away, 25 October. I used that as an issue of interest and asked him what he would like for his birthday. Instead of answering my question about the gift, Davis turned to my little sister and asked her how old my dog was. I felt gutted. They were clearly avoiding me. It was not my imagination.

It was about twenty minutes to midnight when they told everyone that they wanted to go home. I offered to take them to Howlington on the bus with Julia and Joleen. They said clear, "Not you. Only Julia and Joleen."

Not just what they said, but even the way they said, "not you," hurt. My mum also said that I was not allowed. I took no notice of my mum and still went. I was determined to get to the bottom of whatever the story was. We jumped onto the S4 bus. Even on the bus, they only talked to Julia and Joleen, totally ignoring me.

Then Davis said something, I realised was not quite right. "That's not totally true," I butted in calmly.

"We are not talking to you, little liar!" Davis said.

"What are you talking about?" I asked. "Why do you call me a liar?"

"Little soft pimple you are," was Noel's response. "You cannot even tell the truth about your own age! You want to be older than you really are. You just want to put us in trouble!"

"That's why we do not want anything to do with you," Davis added, turning to Joleen. "You should not hang around with her. She is just a silly suckling baby."

I did not give Joleen a chance to answer but said something that I regretted later. Davis continued having a go at me, and it ended up with us three shouting angrily at each other. The bus driver slowed down and told us all to shut up or go down that very minute. He was a chunky, heavily built bouncer of a driver. I bet you, Sara, he probably went to the gym pumping iron all day when he is off work. We all froze and apologised.

Actually, it should have been me apologising as the boys had discovered my long held lie. You see when we first met the boys, I was with a certain girl, Agnes, who preferred to be called Ginnie. They were good-looking boys, who reminded us of most male muscular R&B artists. When we saw them coming towards us at a bus stop, Ginnie said to me, "Golly! There comes company to go clubbing with."

Well and truly, they did ask us if we wanted to go clubbing with them. Cautious about child abuse cases, which lately social workers had been raving about in the area, the boys asked our ages. Ginnie diverted the question by asking them their respective birthdays first. I did not know why she did that, but she winked at me while talking.

After giving their birthdays, they repeated the question.

"I am eighteen and Taxina is seventeen," immediately answered Ginnie, who was 17 at the time. She quickly winked at me again as she responded.

I had just turned twelve but looked well over sixteen, with my chest treasury jutting out of my tight bras. My Brazilian looking 32A papaya boobs actually embarrassingly commanded more male attention than some celebrities' breasts did. I got Ginnie's hint and added that I had just celebrated my seventeenth birthday the previous weekend.

We hit the drinking joint and had one of the best nights, going home totally pissed. Two nights later, Dominic, one of the boys, and I fell in love. That was the first time I fell in love and it was because I said I was seventeen. Now the boys had found out that I had lied about my age. To this day, I still do not know how.

Off the bus, Davis and Noel said good-bye to everyone else apart from me. "I am sorry guys!" I tried shouting amid sobs. "I didn't mean to hurt anyone!"

The boys just went, as if they did not hear me.

I told Julia and Joleen what had happened a year earlier. That night, when I got home, my little sister was, fortunately, already fast asleep. I lay down and cried myself to sleep.

Two months passed before I got back in contact with Davis and Noel. One night Noel, Vin, Chris, and Dominic were going out clubbing. So Davis, Joleen, and I decided to walk to Wimbledon and back, getting pissed. And get pissed we did.

As we walked back around midnight, we saw a wide beam of light and suddenly a car pulled over. It was Vin's car with all the other boys in it. I decided to walk away as I had not made up with Davis. Vin, and Chris, and I did not even have a clue about where I stood with Dom.

I could hear Dom making a silly noise and saying to Davis, "How could you…" Davis then came over and said that Noel and Dominic were going to come with us.

"Whatever," I said. "I am going to be walking ahead anyway." You see, Sara, I deeply loved Dominic, and we had been seeing each other up until he found out my true age. I was completely broken hearted. I would talk about Dom 24/7 to my friends, especially Julia. When on my own in my room, I cried over him hours on end.

It felt so horrible to be dumped just for age, a number that no one actually sees. He had switched himself off so easily. I loved him, but he did not love me back. I even considered killing myself with some of my mum's sleeping tablets because I loved him so much. Nothing else held any meaning, and I thought and believed that no one could ever replace him. Was I right?

Back to the story. It was time for us all to go our separate ways. It was time to each try our respective luck at some other dreams. I kept walking and said goodbye to Davis and Noel. I naively thought I would not see Dominic's face, but I did. He walked a lot faster on purpose, came very close to me, as if passing, and leaned right into my face. He made sure to show me his disappointed look on his face. I understood, because if anyone had known he was going out with a thirteen-year-old, he would surely have been locked up.

I suddenly burst into tears as Dominic walked on past. Noel and Joleen came up to me and caringly ruffled my hair, which was flowing over my shoulders.

"So you are not going back to their yard then?" I asked Noel, trying to control my sobs.

"No," Noel replied. "I am going to walk you two to the bus stop and go to my house."

I cried on for some paces, as the two tried comforting me. We then caught the bus and went home. From that day on I kept going up to Tooting, but only when I was sure that Dominic was not there. I kept going there because, looking at the familiar buildings, I could relieve the nice moments that I had shared with Dominic there. I smelled the roses again and sat under some trees. But this time, the smell was not as sweet without Dom. Sitting under the huge trees was now a lonely exercise.

Since then I started going with Julia. We would each buy an ice cream and sit and eat on the bus stop, chatting away. We soon hooked up with another group of boys of a different type altogether. I loved chatting away with the boys on that bus stop. One of them was so funny, each time he cracked jokes we were in stitches with laughter.

Anyway, on one of our visits to Tooting, I thought of a dream book. So I started writing about Dominic and me and how our life together would have been had he not flinched over my age. We had talked about how many children we were going to have and what their names were going to be. I had also written him a lot of letters and poems.

That day, I had told Davis and Noel about the letters and poems. They told me to give them to Dominic. While I repeatedly declined, they persuaded me, and I ended giving Dominic the letters I wrote, but I kept the love poems.

The next day I got a phone call and it was Dominic himself.

He said to me, "Oh, Taxie, thank you so much. You don't know how I cried last night. I actually cried myself to sleep. I did not know you loved me that much, and I wish I had loved you even better in return. I am sorry."

He said that we unfortunately could not be together anymore, at least not until I reached seventeen, if we still felt for each other. He made it clear that he loved me, but my age made things difficult for him.

I thanked him, and it really pleased me to know that he loved my letters and that he loved me as a person. I slowly learned to accept our parting, and two years later, I totally stopped having feelings for him. He, however, kept flirting with me, but I reminded him I was forbidden fruit.

As months passed, I somehow loved the bus stop group of boys and realised that one of them actually lived near me as we boarded the same bus going home. Surprise, surprise, it was the joker. We started sitting on the same seat and would joke together all the way home.

I stopped going down to Tooting and now just spoke to the Tooting lot on the phone. As for the joker, the jokes started becoming flirty.

One day not long ago, I said to Julia: "Haven't you noticed that I have stopped crying over and talking about Dominic?"

"Oh, yea," Julia said. "That's definitely good for you. Do I seem to see that you are getting closer to our joking prince or is it my imagination?"

"Oh, you mean Gregory?" I asked, owning up. "I guess he is better than Dominic, at least he makes me cry with laughter."

One day, on my way from Tooting, I shared a seat with this joker. He started joking about the programmes on TV from the day before. He actually could make good impressions, acting and talking like Jeremy Kyle on the show, especially the part when he tells off hopeless couples who cannot tell their heads from their tails.

"Outa my show, the two of yea. Here I am wasting time and advice when there are lots out there looking for love. It is life we are talking, love, not a rehearsal. Out you go, and good luck for both of ya, with your wrong choices!"

The entire bus was in stitches and my side ached with laughing. As I steadied myself and wiped my tears from laughter, I found my hand in his. Normally I would have withdrawn it, but I felt very comfortable and was honestly enjoying his touch. I loved it.

Yes one of the boys, the one that joked a lot, actually had been watching me for some time. He later told me that at first I looked grumpy and not so interesting. But then, when I laughed, I made his day. He was very much different from Dominic, who tore my heart apart and made me cry with cruelty. That was the very truth.

Well exit Dominic. Enter Gregory.

When the Tooting lot started fussing about my age and made me cry, Dominic must have thought that time would stand still. Well, time did not stand still. Nature rearranges itself and no one should think after years that they can start where they left off. For love can be a fast train, if you let it. More so, especially if you try and fill your moments with laughter!

You see, during the period I was crying, Gregory saw me as not so attractive. As soon as I started laughing, I attracted those like Gregory in the dozens. Now I am moving on and, so long as Dominic is happy with himself—that is all that matters after all. I know that I still have some love for him, but I need to move on.

To cut the story short, Gregory and I are now in love. For me the future is Gregory.

He is the way forward. I love him and he loves me. I am in probably the best relationship ever. It feels good too. This time it must last forever.

So you see Sara, when I lost Dominic, for no real fault of mine, I thought I was the most unlucky girl in the world. Since January of last year, I have moved on and I am definitely the luckiest girl in the world. I know that Gregory has never been bothered by my age. He says that he loves me so much that if it meant that he had to wait he would have waited for as long as it would take the world to recognize me as a woman.

A lot of things have happened to me, and I have difficulties trusting anyone anymore. When I do, though, I give it my all. It took me a long time to trust my boyfriend, Gregory, but now I do. I shall try hard and not ruin it myself with my own insecurities.

Seriously, Sara, I thank my stars and the good Lord for blessing me with the most trustworthy, caring, sharing, thoughtfully forgiving, and kindest boyfriend that anyone could ever wish for.

Back to your disappointment. If that frog—for that is what he really was—ever loved you, he would not have hurt you. Well at least he would have apologised and made up for treating you roughly. But did he? Now go figure it out girl.

He wanted you to go bananas, walking about all day in pyjamas! I bet it would make his day seeing you in that state, knowing that not even a competitor will want a zombie for a princess.

But you sort yourself out, girl. Make the best of the agony aunties. You never know what prince is on the lookout for you. You see, there is a future after every disappointment. Even after the sharpest bend, the road does continue, only in a different direction. Our job is to find that new direction.

How about that, Sara? Did that not make you feel better? You are not alone and have never been. Stop crying and start living. Among all the frogs out there, there are some princes looking for a starry eyed girl like you. As Dolly Parton said, "You'd better get to living, giving, be willing and forgiving, cause all healing has to start with you."

You better stop whining and pining, and get your dreams in line. Then, just shine, design, refine, until they come true. Be a little more willing' to make a better way. Don't sweat the small stuff, keep your chin up, and just hang tough. And if it gets too rough, fall on your knees and pray, and do that every day. Like I did. Share your dreams and share your laughter, for when you laugh, the world laughs with you.

Well, enjoy your day Sara, and I hope to hear from you soon.

Taxie XXX

CHAPTER 10

Did You Know I am your Juliet?

Candle Mews,
Radnor-cliff crescent
Folkestone,
CT20 2JQ

Today's date

Dear Greg,

This may be an unusual letter to you, considering that I could simply have flashed you, and you would have called me back. I know as usual, with your free weekend minutes, we would have talked until the cows come home. That's the beauty of T-Mobile. Well maybe, unless you have an O_2 SIM card as I hear they have their own sweet deals. I am actually tempted to switch over, but with all the marketing traps, I really cannot make up my mind.

Anyway, because I have always wanted to write you this long letter, I now want to let you in on some treasured memories, ideas, concerns, and dreams. Do understand, Greg, I do love you and enjoy talking to you. In addition, I do enjoy listening to your sweet voice, it's the sweetest sound. Your name makes the sweetest music, better sounding than the mellowest violin and more soothing than the best classical music.

This creates a problem for me for when I am in your presence. I cannot think and talk fast and long enough. Call it err, ooh, vee, vee, ee. Whenever we meet, a kiss and a cuddle, and you want us to talk. I know you have endless funny stories and jokes, I must add, some of them are imaginary I guess. However, my knees go wobbly, probably unnerved by your voice, which sounds like Orpheus' enchantment. All I want to do is sit by your side, hold your hand, cuddle up, and listen to you tell me sweet nothings forever.

I know I love you Greg, and I know that I sound confusing. I don't appear to be so emotionally all over you, other than just sitting there and listening to you talk. The reality is that I have always been ashamed of my life and my experiences in care. I feel so worthless and undeserving of your love and attention.

Yes, you do repeatedly remind me that you love me for who I am and not where I am, nor my family or my background, and I love to hear that. I do listen when you say that I do not have to win any trophies to be yours, that I just have to remain myself, providing comfort and baking cakes and stuff. You tell me that I need not be a super girl, immaculate in all silly attributes, that I only need to hold the promise to be the golden mother of your babies. By the way, I do hope and believe I will do better than Shrek's Fiona!

However, the trouble is that, unlike the other girls, my background troubles me. I always wish I could wish it away or make it different. Really, what troubles me is that people who know about it judge me based on it, instead of who I am and what I can do now. I love you and will always give you my love, forever. Maybe even forever is not long enough to give you all my love.

Oh Greg, you will never know how much I really love you and how much I miss you. I really do wish we had gone to the same schools and sat in the same class on the same desk. Then, you could pinch me if I were naughty.

Actually, I would never be naughty in class at all, not with you around. It would be too embarrassing. I would also be learning very well. I would have been super focused. What need would I have to dream about you when I have you around? Of course, if we would have had detentions every week I am not sure I would have been able to keep my hands to myself!

You know sometimes I have one of those teachers that go on and on, talking almost to themselves. They treat you as if you are not there. Then I do switch off and start dreaming about holding and squeezing the hand of my dear Greg. The teacher catches me by asking, "Is it true Taxie?"

And I always reply, "Yes sir, it is true," hoping he leaves it there.

"What's true?" he queries on.

I then wake up and own up. "I am sorry sir. I was a bit lost."

"Pay attention, then," he says, continuing with the topic.

Soon after, it becomes boring again and I start writing you love poems on the inside cover of my notebooks. When I get home in the evening, I transfer them onto the cards which I put in the special card holder by date. Sometimes when I am bored at our residential home, I go upstairs to my room. I put your photograph on the dressing table and read the poems out to you, with Mariah Carey or Toni Braxton playing softly in the background.

I then wash my hair and tie it in a pony tail, just the way you say you like it. But soon I tire of that and let my hair down, let it flow all over my shoulders, and give you a good-night call. Or sometimes I send you one of those confusing texts that make you call me immediately. Then, I can tell you sweet nothings, while enjoying the sound of your heavy breathing over the phone from a distance.

Did you ever know that whenever we talk I put the phone on recording mode? I do. That way, each time I feel lonely, I simply replay our chats, and there we, love forever like two wild pigeons. Replaying those chats gives me strength enough to carry on. Other than that, every day that I live here in the children's residential home is an empty day.

Did you know that residents here are not the worst children in the country, yet residential homes are the last resort? They are unseemly refugee homes for stranded children whom local authorities have not really prioritised for fostering. So yes, laden with that background knowledge, life here can be empty. The only exceptions are the days that I have a one-on-one tuition, evenings in which I go horse riding. You know I really was into horse riding, but I have had to accept it as an alternative to endless boredom.

There are times that I become cross with staff and really lose my cool. This may be over some silly comments that someone made or simply because one misplaced my bra when they removed laundry from the drier. I then stomp off to my room in anger so hot it could char the culprit alive were they to enter my heart at the time.

"Come and tell me," Jennifer calls, knocking on my door.

"Go away," I shout back, "and leave me alone!"

"What's wrong, Taxina?"

She never gives up so easily. No, that Jennie doesn't.

"Whatever," I retort. "Now clear off!"

She goes away, but I know that she is awaiting the opportune time to ask me again. When she is on shift, she never goes home leaving me sulky at all. I must admit that she makes me feel loved sometimes. When she is gone, I draw the curtains, get into bed, and sob myself to sleep. Later on, I realise that I was not really angry with Jennie but with everybody that participated in messing up my life.

Then, I think about you. You see, Gregory, you are the love of my life, my dream, and yes, the apple of my eye. You give me a sense of security, and you remind me of my dad. I have not seen him for two years, and my mum does not want me to know where he is. She will not even let us talk about it. That drives me mad! If ever she had any problems with her dad, I never had any with my dad. I will always hold her responsible for my misery.

Instead of using her love for him, if she had any, she used it to steer him away from whatever she did not like him doing. She shopped him to coppers two and a half years ago. I may not be as experienced as her, but I believe if I did not like whatever you are doing, Greg, I can love you away from it. I can cry for and with you until you see your folly and how much it may cost us. But that's me, Taxie, thinking. I can say that my mum is one of the only two silly old cows I have known in my life. Yes, she is, if you ask me.

Surprisingly, even the social worker, who is supposed well-informed about families, never talks about my dad. She is always, "Your mum this... Your mum that... Eh, your mum veh, veh, veh."

I feel like shouting at them all: "You silly lot, I miss my daddy!" Where and how my dad is doing is all I care to know.

In class, if I am not daydreaming about you, I am daydreaming about Dad, especially around Christmas and birthdays. He used to play his mouth organ and could even play every latest song, even R&B, rapping all the way while distributing cakes. Sometimes he would surprise my sister and me by dressing up like Santa on Christmas morning. As you can imagine, I have had empty Christmases since.

You know, I have never told you these things because I did not want you to feel guilty or challenged, or believe that I want you to measure up to my dad. I love you Greg, and all I want to hear is that you love me. I can never hear enough of that, not even forever is long enough for me to keep hearing the three words. They make me forget the dark days and shine me forward.

Really these sweet nothings do matter. They are the parachute of our love. Never believe the celebrities when they say they need no parachute, as you can see them all stumbling out of love one by one, wallowing in misery. Why? They stop talking tenderly, lose the magic, and don't recognise their folly. They go in all the wrong places, searching for new love. Let's love each other forever, Gregory. What's this life for if not loving?

Listen Gregory, you need to be strong, as I shall count on you to help me grow above my own thinking, attitude, and esteem. Do please help me accept that I can be better than my care-home reputation, better and higher than the low expectations that the general community seems to have about looked after children.

Greg, my love, your name is sweet and so reassuring. For once, yesterday I went to the library and, looking at your picture on the phone, I thought of looking up the meaning of your name on the internet. Yes it is a sweet lovely name. I am not sure you know that it means someone who loves company. "Gregarius" it is, I think. Much like gregarious as an English adjective, coming from Latin like the Gregorian chant we once heard from Mrs Pinky Pie in religious education class.

Talking about being gregarious, I have been dreaming about us starting a family. Maybe we'll do so in nine years' time, when I am 24 and you are 27. I shall have your four babies, two girls and two boys. All little "Gregorys," chattering, yelling, and driving us mad, mirrors of ourselves. Then, you can indeed be gregarious according to your own name.

Thinking about you and your voice inspires me so much that I feel that everything is possible. I develop so much energy that I really can do anything. I do hope and wish that by then I shall be Mrs Link the lawyer, or Mrs Link the heart surgeon, while you are the exceptional aeroplane engineer, naming your own hourly wage. I can already see us flying to Barbados, Hawaii, or seeing a herd of zebras in Kenya or having a tropical dinner on Table Mountain in South Africa, while listening to Zulus chanting. Maybe we could even have a holiday resort of our own in St. Lucia. Think about it Greg! Rich dreams are something to keep us going.

If we stick at it Gregory, as my dad used to say, we can make it. By the way, this should not disturb you. I do admire and envy you. Both your parents are well educated and earning comfortable figures. I think of your mum, being a lawyer, as an exceptional woman. I know she may be pleased to know that I admire her. But please don't tell her that I used to smoke weed, as you may break her heart.

Gregory, let us work hard, finish our education, and get jobs or create jobs that shall allow us freedom. We need freedom to own a house and peacefully sleep in it with no fear of mortgage payments.

Let's us stick together, loving forever, and no child of ours shall ever have to end up in a care. Life in care is meant to be supportive, but it is unnatural. It is hard. It is bad. Even when you are fostered, yours are the dregs of love. Whatever emotional remains after your foster parents have loved their biological children is what you get.

You know I love drawing but lately my pictures have been rather sad, affected by how I feel about being in care. My current pictures reflect my fears and frustrations about the future. There are times when I am excited about what the future holds, but most of the time, I am scared of not being equipped with enough survival skills to live on my own.

Today, I drew one such sad picture that says so much—the stuff Elton John sings about in sad songs. Today, I really felt sad. Here, let me reproduce for you the write up I wanted to text you. Obviously, I could not as it is too long for a text.

Things in my life change every day. Good things change into bad and bad things change into good. I have had a lot of bad patches lately. Of course I have had good times, too, but I mostly remember bad ones. Not that I enjoy feeling bad; I do not.

I need to be, and I am, grateful to everyone involved with my life, everyone who has enabled me to have the fun and excitement that I have had. Maybe I have had much more fun compared to the average girl of my age. But sometimes I do not even consider it fun at all.

You know when someone is getting you into something to make you forget about something else? Such are the days when they make me go horse riding. It can be fun when you want it to be, but not when they make it an obvious substitute. Little do they know how easy it is to focus on something in your mind while safely galloping!

Then, my heart misses a beat, and I become alive when you call me or when I imagine holding your hand. I guess this is what people talk about when they say that they are desperately falling head over heels.

Isn't it strange that hate is the other side of love, laughter the other side of crying, living the other side of dying, and light is the other side of darkness? So why are we so worried, sometimes, when the choices in life always come in twos?

My life is like a book. Every page in it tells its own different part of my life. I have had the luck of having lasting mates, especially those I knew before going into care, such as Joleen, who is like a sister to me. Whenever I am worried, I ring Joleen up and spill out my heart. She is very understanding and lets me talk and only makes few comments, at the end of our conversations, I feel like I have had a hot shower, with all my troubles washed away.

Of course Greg you may be wondering why I do not phone you instead. It is because I do not want to overload you with my worries. I love you too much to burden you with my silly girlie concerns when you have your boyish ones to think about it. To be honest, I did not think that you would understand my problems as your family is well off, both socially and financially.

Joleen is someone who, although slightly older than I am, has been through a road as rough as mine. She is one lucky burger, a reformed junky, who is now well reunited with her family. She understands about being cared for and the deep emptiness that sometimes overwhelms one in care.

You and your family all appear to understand one another. For example, each time that I see your dad, my eyes fill up with tears. He reminds me of my own. I have not seen my dad for the three years. I do not know if he is alive or dead. My mother does not want to know. She just cannot be asked. But that is a different story.

Next week, I am leaving for a new children's home. It is called Wishhouse, but don't ask me why it is called this.

I see you raising your eyebrows. "New?" New to me, bugger! Not new in existence, of course. I am going to be in this new home for two weeks, and then I go back home to Mum's. She and everyone else believe that she is rehabilitated and well away from her druggie past and that all shall be well between us.

No Greg. Don't just agree. Mum may be back from the rehab clinic and all the rest of herself management life skills courses, but how is she going to cope with life when she still sees that same poisonous boyfriend of hers? He himself uses and peddles drugs.

Who in their right mind thought they were helping Mum recover while ignoring her emotional peg? He too should have gone into rehabilitation and trained for a new, decent job. That's what I would have told him if I was Mum, even though I am struggling with my own little demons.

Why not train as a plumber or painter and be honestly minted, rather than mess up the lives of others? He uses Mum. That man does. Hungry for love, poor Mum has become his kitten. That is the home I am supposed to return to. It may be true that there is a turn and a time for everything, but I am scared. I am so, so, so scared Greg. However, I cannot say no, for I did agree that I would return home if Mum went through rehabilitation. If only she had kicked her predator bastard out!

I guess it's Hobson's choice, squashed between a thirty-tonner truck and the Eurotunnel wall, the care system that ignores my frustrations and the deep blue sea with an unfathomed bottom of unknowns. I have to try and think it's all fine.

Adding to my fears of domestic insecurity is the fact that I have begun to like the country side of Kent. I love the gardens, and the expansive fields have been creeping on me unaware, pretty much like the white hair that attacked my dad's forehead. Somehow, I am not really looking forward to the London atmosphere. There does not seem to be anywhere to go where one can think beyond the trouble in the parking lots, shop fronts, tube stations, and street corners.

The other day, I went to see Mum's friend at Honslow, near Heathrow. I remember having visited the area when I was about seven. Then, I remember some streets being lined with huge trees that bloomed with lots of pretty flowers in spring. The air was live with the fresh sweet-smelling fragrance of flowers.

What did we see on this recent trip? Huge jumbo planes on a new runway. That reminded of one of the new developments at Saint Pancreas. That is the new terminal for fast trains that go to and from the continent. The endless construction work is eating the remainder of whatever free space we had to play on as children. The new flats and towering business buildings seem to kiss the sky. They now make the sunrise take longer than it took before. They also make it set more swiftly, when it is not covered in smog that is.

All the grass one sees now is artificially-grown turf. Even foxes now lose the natural colour of their coats, testifying to the ever-increasing fumes that give me migraines. You know, Greg, here in Kent, I hardly have a headache. Yet in London, if I am not having a hangover headache or recovering from stoning, it is a migraine from car fumes. The ever-increasing number of cars and their frequency on the roads make it impossible to even sit by the roadside and enjoy an ice cream like we used to.

This is well possible here in Kent, at least in most parts of it. Here, you can sit in the park and dream yourself away without undue fear of rapists or muggers. You can watch the sun and the moon rise and enjoy the splendour of the sun as it sets. Yes, these are parts of the memories I must carry with me home to Mum, that empty home. Gregory, I am scared, so, so scared.

You know what, Greg? The bosses at my current home, supported by my dozy social worker who cannot see beyond her nose, say that Mum can take me to live with one of her friends if I do not feel comfortable at her place. Displacement after displacement. How does anyone expect me to be comfortable at anyone else's house if I cannot be comfortable at Mum's?

Why even take me out of care at all, especially now, when I have GCSEs on my mind? I have been making a lot of progress with one-to-one tuition, and they have planned that I join a new school in Carshalton. How can I join a new school, live with a new family although friends of my mum, and pass my exams? Man, give me a break!

But Greg I can only say this to you. At my current home, no one would listen to me. This is why I am writing to you today, Greg. Do please stand by me. I need a supporting shoulder. I do not really know what to do in the next two weeks; my life is in a daze.

On a lighter note, did you ever know how we met? Do you know my side of the meeting story? Or to make it a puzzle, do you know Juliet, Romeo's girlfriend? Watch out for my next letter. By way of concluding this one, remember that I appreciate your love and dedication to me. I love having you by my side. Please keep loving me the way that I love you loving me.

My heart smiles and chants a melody to which only you can give words. It is making music to the endless dreams beyond the crossroads of life. Say my name, and my heart shall respond. For in love, my independence yearns for dependence. My freedom creates loneliness, leaving me a yearning for the way things should have been. I am talking about the way things should have been, had my dad not been shopped. Yes, had I not been allotted life in care. You are my Romeo, and I am your Juliet forever.

Taxie XXX

CHAPTER 11

Mummie, Is this Your Daughter?

Candle Mews,
Radnor-cliff crescent
Folkestone,
CT20 2JQ

Today's date

Dear Mum,

This morning I woke up feeling very down, very dry in my mouth. It is a feeling you probably shall never experience and can never identify with. It is a feeling associated with loneliness and substitutes that do not last.

It is a Monday, and you shall remember that I only returned last night from visiting you and my dear little sister Amy. I cannot place my finger on it, Mummy, but when I come to see you, to visit you, I do not seem to find what I want. I do not seem to enjoy the visit. I guess because all I share is a meal.

You are engrossed in your own problems and my little sister has a litany of her own that I cannot help but listen to, and I do. But to my problems? No one listens, as you surely don't.

I know you faintly want to listen, but from the blank distant look on your face, you do not. Therefore, I stop trying to make you listen. I stop trying to talk to you and share with you something about myself and all the questions I wish someone would help me to answer. I may have been very young when I last saw my dad, but he did listen to me, even when he hugged me and said nothing.

From the discussion I had with Amy, you seem to pay more attention to Ben, your boyfriend, than to us, both when he comes around and even when you are alone. Tragically, you seem to miss him more than he misses you. Unknowingly perhaps, you ignore us, yet even when he is around, he makes you ignore us even more.

I keep being told in the home that if I cannot be with the one I love, I must love the one I am with. Maybe you need to realise that your bond to us, your little children is and needs to be stronger than you can ever have with any other man besides our dad. Do you ever realise, Mum, that by ignoring us like that you make us hate Ben and any boyfriend you may ever have who makes us compete for your attention and love? In simple terms, you create rivalry.

You can choose your boyfriends if you really want to, but we cannot choose. And we did not choose our mummy, did we? I was just wondering if you were to choose a mummy for us, what kind of a mummy would you have chosen?

Mummy, I know that you have your own needs that I cannot meet, as I have been reminded repeatedly by my carers. I know that you need a life, romance, and action, but you also need some tranquillity, a life of peace brought by some time with two contented daughters and not the falsehood of drugs. Maybe you need to learn to love us again, to enjoy each moment with the company you have, Amy and I, your two little angels, as you used to call us in spite of our blemishes.

There is the unkind reminder of reality. Living in care has shot me into the world of adulthood even before I was mentally and physically mature. I therefore know that you may soon miss us. As per your beloved Mike and the Mechanics' song, "The Living Years," it may soon be too late, we might be beyond your living world socially. I already can see that Amy is not the little princess I knew a year ago.

With bigger boobs and girlie celebrities—the Jordans and Kate Mosses of this world—staring at a growing girl from the front of every magazines, comes more mischief, unpredictability, and confusing attention from men. In the absence of Dad, who do we talk to when you are distant, even when you physically are sitting next to us?

Mum, if you do not give us attention, you can be sure that we will look for it elsewhere, even with painful consequences.

You probably would not even have guessed it. When I told you that I was going to see Greg, my boyfriend, I first went to meet my gangmates, Garry and the Crew. We drank and smoked weed. Skunk doesn't help, I know. But it makes me feel better for the moment, a quick refuge from the emotional rejection of you, Mum.

It stops me from off-loading my frustrations on innocent Greg, my poor prince who hates my smoking but loves me in spite of it. It stops me from smacking Vicky for stroking my hair, when actually she is only being a loving sister.

I use skunk because it makes me feel good. But to be honest, no one should take the stuff as it is bad and often has me stoned senseless.

You never knew I can pick locks, did you? Did you know that your daughter can hot-wire cars? I try every waking hour to find a last way to connect to you.

You shall never know I can fire revolvers and know where to negotiate and buy ammunition rounds by the size of the machine. "All that for a girl of 14?" you ask yourself. I did not intend to break your heart, but you must know that all these are the fruits of you failing to give us loving attention. This just shows you how far you are from your own daughter.

As for the gangmates, all it took was one evening of snogging DK, the boss, and nothing more. From then on, all the boys respected me with fear. DK also has to do as I say or his wife will know he snogged me. He also respects Greg. In public, we just pose as old, good mates. DK's boys give me spliff when I need it. Greg does not like it and wishes I would stop using it. I know he loves me and I honestly hope someday I will stop. It's just that without your support, Mum, I just can't help myself. Besides Greg, what do I have to live for anyway?

As I write this letter, I am sitting by the window of my room, directly facing a huge cherry tree. Every morning, when I open the curtains, I see a brown squirrel that is patched white all over her back. I have never seen her with her family and no mates ever come to visit her. I have since made her my mate and have called her "Gringo."

I throw some bread crumbs and Gringo comes down the tree and picks them up with two front paws, while standing on hind legs. It is a lovely sight to see, but Gringo appears lonely. Being an albino squirrel probably means she is rejected by her mates. Being in care, Mum, I feel like Gringo.

I know I fell in love with Greg at an early age, too young to be sensible, probably like Juliet and Romeo. But this is what happens when one is fumbling in the dark looking for something to provide emotional security. Rightly said, I fell in love and not walked into love. While I love Greg, I think he loves me more than I do.

He is totally open with me, yet I hide loads of secrets from him. The fact that he loves me in spite of knowing the kind of mum you are, knowing that I take skunk, and the fact that all his family is well educated and financially well off, tells me that I do not deserve him. He has such a happy family, Mum.

Each time I visit him reminds me of the happy days we had: you, me, my little sister, and Daddy, before the dark days of Carshalton. I think of the days we would walk into the park and have picnics. Did you realise that your cheating on Dad while he was in prison actually took away the little hope we had of him returning home? It was the last straw that confirmed to him that no woman can ever be trusted. Not after the way his own mother short-changed him, conning him out of his own inheritance.

The proverbial biblical Rebeccas of this world make me regret being born a woman. You know well that Grandma sold off her own house and all three properties that she had been entrusted with for the children by her husband. She did that without informing Dad, her eldest child, who only heard about the sell the day the new owners served them notice to leave the house. You were the only woman he had left to trust, and look at what you did to him. Other than me and my little sister, what hope does he have in this life?

You have tried to take refuge in drugs, but have they helped? Especially after the man who helped you wreck your family tossed you away for a younger beauty? Has any of your new loves really brought you lasting happiness?

By watching Gringo the albino squirrel from my window, I am learning that I will become happiest by looking outside and picking a beautiful spot on which to concentrate. Sometimes, I see the same flowers I have been looking at before and find them particularly pretty. I am sure that the flowers have not changed, but my focus has.

On my thirteenth birthday, when Doreen, my key worker, bought me the trendiest and most expensive shoes, which I wanted. I hardly noticed. They still mean nothing to me because she gave them to me on a day I was terribly upset by the hogging behaviour of your current boyfriend. Yet watching Gringo makes me smile.

This is my constant reminder that my happiness comes from inside me and from the simple things. Gringo has no idea at all that her presence or jumping antics make me smile. At such a time, I mentally leave my body, never conscious of where I am standing or what I am wearing, not even whether I have eaten or not. I go out there and play with Gringo and start my day happily. All from inside my mind.

Therefore, it appears, Mummy, that our happiness cannot really come from outside. Not really. Not from people who pretend to love us, nor from any possessions, no matter how new or expensive.

I am your daughter, hardly sixteen, but I have experimented enough with drugs, skunk, and casual love to know that they do hurt. Right now, with all the drinks and weed, I can hardly concentrate and I told my tutor so. He is very overbearing and lets me cry my heart out, and still he reminds me that I have a chance to rebuild my life. He says everyone can choose a dream to work towards, no matter how bleak their circumstances appear.

Mummy, I need you to help me achieve my dream. But you are no use if you still belief in the solace of drugs. Mummy I love you, but I feel like "sugar in tea" after all the spliff of yesterday. I have let my private tutor down, but that is because I was let down by you. I did not want my little sister to see me crying for you. I may not come home for the next three weeks as my visit to you does not help at all. I want to try and break my destructive habits, pass my GCSE, and be an exemplary example for my little sister.

It would be nice to grow up in a family. But for now, I must live in this machine-planned, business run place that they call my "home." I do hope that Amy grows up in a better environment than the one where I am growing up. I do hope that Daddy is alive and well somewhere. I do hope that you learn soon that we are your priceless treasures and that you owe us, and yourself, some realistic love. I do love you Mummy.

Taxie XXX

CHAPTER 12

You Really Want to Walk in My Shoes?

Candle Mews,
Radnor-cliff crescent
Folkestone,
CT20 2JQ

Today's date

Dear Other Children,

I see you happily playing with your parents and siblings. I see some of you throw tantrums, bang doors, and shout, "I hate you!" at your mothers just because she said no to an ice cream or asked you to clean up after yourselves. I hear you cursing under your breath when your dad asks you to clean the bathroom or even your own room. I see it in some of your faces, thinking that because your parents say no to everything, they do not love you. I know what you are saying and I feel for you. I therefore have a message for you.

I am one of you, like some of you, I am fifteen. While I have probably been exposed to the adult world, to lots of things and activities, deep down I have an unspent childhood. I am a little girl still yearning for my lost world of innocence and careless freedom. I yearn for days when I could run to my daddy and hold his hand and feel comfortable even when he said nothing to me, days of worry about neither yesterday nor tomorrow. But for me, that life is long gone.

You see, I live in care and have lived that way for the last four years, having gone in just after my tenth birthday. I took myself into care after my father was imprisoned and never came back. My world fell apart as I watched different men walk into our house, and Mum let them into my dad's bedroom. One of them had even taken liberties with me when Mummy and my little sister had gone to the shop. Mum did not believe me.

Then, I watched Mum spend my daddy's hard earned money on frivolous shopping and cocaine. I could not stop fighting with Mum over her leaving my little sister to me with hardly enough food for the day while she went out drinking with her new (every time) boyfriends, most of whom may as well be paedophiles that should have been drowned in the Thames.

So I asked myself, "How can I stretch this limited food to last for days for both my sister and me?" I asked myself that question more often and never had a realistic answer. We were made to put on pairs of jeans from charity shops because they went unnoticed as dirty even if worn for days on end.

Quickly, I realised that the freedom and sense of peace I had when Daddy was around was gone forever. You see, my sister loves eating and loves varieties of food, although she still remains skinny. Sainsbury's Shop was just around a corner, less than a mile from our house. Whenever Mum did not give us enough money to buy food, my little sister always said she would sneak into Sainsbury's and help herself, that she had done it with her friend one day on her way from school and had not been caught.

If the behaviour of my mum did not change, we would soon be on the streets, and the thought of my little sister shoplifting disgusted me. I had recently read about a ten-year-old girl who stole some chocolates from a shop and was caught. Being without her mum, the shop owners threatened to take her to the police. She cried her eyes out, and they made her stand near the shop entrance with a big sign on her neck saying " I am a miserable shoplifter."

The girl would not say where she lived or who her parents were. So they called the police and the police took her away. However, I also understand that the shop keeper was also arrested for traumatising the little girl with that board in spite of her stealing. I dreaded imagining my little sister being that girl.

I remember hearing Daddy telling me that he worked long hours and even weekends, as a van driver in the week and a taxi driver and party organiser on weekends. The van driving kept him away most of the time, but when he did come home, he was always bubbly, filled the food store, fridge, and freezer and made sure our clothes were the right size, clean, and ironed.

He said that we were his two little princesses and he carried our pictures in his wallet. My daddy worked very hard and said he saved money for us and gave his cash point card to Mummy in case we needed something while he was away.

I would wake up early to have a bath and make packed lunches for my sister and myself. After I had finished, I would wake my sister up to have a bath and have breakfast.

"Where is the money Daddy said he was saving for us?" I said to Mummy one morning. You see, we had to go to school and there was no bread or milk in the fridge. This was the day I saw no way of making my packed lunch, let alone fixing breakfast.

"He didn't have any money, love," she replied and walked into the bathroom shutting the door behind her.

"No Mummy, there's got to be some money somewhere," I went on. "Daddy always worked long hours and you kept his cash point card remember?"

But Mummy did not answer. As she came out of the bathroom, her eyes looked red and watery. She just passed me and went upstairs to her room. That was a sign that she had gone sniffing her drugs again.

Anger welled up in me. She had probably blown Daddy's money on drugs. I remembered that I had been keeping a pound a week from the pocket money Daddy had been giving me. I had a good fifty pounds in one of my earliest purses I kept under the bed. I took it, went to buy all the groceries we needed for the week, and gave a fiver to my sister. I told my sister that I would be late from school that day, but that she should not tell Mummy, not that she would care anyway, but I did not want her upset.

We needed help, but I did not know where to turn. I still do not know the full story as to why Daddy had to go to prison. Mummy does not want to talk about it and she makes me think that he might have fought with her many boyfriends and hurt the other bloke or something.

Daddy had some mates he called his brothers, but these Uncles Bill and Dan stopped coming round to see us soon after Daddy went to prison. I hoped one of these men could give me some idea of where exactly Daddy was and maybe how he intended us to survive in his absence.

After school, I walked to Riverside garages where Uncle Danny had said he worked driving a forklift. I asked if he was around but was told that he had left and gone away for a new job. I asked if anyone had his phone number, but they said no. No one even seemed to know who Uncle Bill was. To my understanding, he had been a friend to Uncle Dan. I had hit a dead end.

The groceries I had bought would not last us forever. I had to act quickly. I slowly realised that the food would probably be sufficient for my sister alone if she looked after it. So I decided to look at the job centre where I understood people who did not have anything to eat signed for some money to live on. When I got there, an elderly woman who attended to me was very kind and listened very carefully. She then made a few phone calls, and in the next ten minutes, another woman I later discovered was a social worker came to collect me to go to another building.

When I went back home, Mum promised to take better care of us. But then a week later, her boyfriend did something nasty to me while Mum and Vicky were out getting groceries. Mum would not believe me, but through her friend, I informed social services. I never went back home from that day and was taken into a children's home, from which I went to school and explained to my sister what I had done.

Looking back, that was probably the biggest error of my life, but again, I sought to bring our plight to some authorities. In any case, the Social Services people would have found out about our situation sooner or later. You see, my fellow children, the situation grew worse. Sometimes, we never had a proper bath before going to school. We put on the same knickers we had worn the day before, and I know that sometimes I smelled of wee. I was embarrassed when boys taunted me and said that I stunk of toilet.

Now five years later, my mum and I are trying very hard to rebuild our relationship. Believe me it is a hard road. I cannot understand how she failed to look after us even when she received benefits to do so. But if you can help it, never ever leave home. Seek for help elsewhere but leaving home is daft.

Forget those cosmetically arranged reunions you see on TV shows. No one knows and feels what goes on inside you when you are alienated from your parents for one reason or another.

I always said to myself that someday I would find a way and bring my experiences and lessons to you. My dear fellow children, remember, I said I am still a child at heart. I wanted to tell you about the world outside your normal home, the world without a mummy and daddy. Have you ever imagined what that would be like? I live that life and it is only half of a life. The other half is filled with wishing that your life were different. After reading this, you may have to think again about those sulky days when you think that your parents are the worst, when you threaten to go away. You may want to rethink how you look at and value your home, siblings, parents, and discipline. For all these things mean you have a loving home. Believe me, I have none of these, and I miss them every day.

As I have no one to send my love to, here then, have from me shiploads of love.

Taxie XXX

CHAPTER 13

Gary Greenhouse:
Whose Children are his Mules?

Candle Mews,
Radnor-cliff crescent
Folkestone,
CT20 2JQ

Today's date

Dear Mr Chancellor,

This morning I had a business studies lesson, and my teacher explained something about how some countries are richer than other countries are. He illustrated how some are perpetual importers, running out of their foreign exchange as they spend it on importing clothes, food, and even cars.

She explained that the difference between the various countries' well-being depended on the development level of their technology, knowledge, and service industries; how shrewd and cautious their banks are; and how meddlesome or reserved they are regarding international politics. She gave the example of Switzerland and Andorra as rich countries that remain low and avoid all political and economic troubles.

As the lesson ended, I was left with many questions. For example, do they have prisons in Switzerland and Andorra? How long is the longest term of stay in their prisons? And what do those prisoners do day in and day out that is nationally constructive?

I have always believed that we, the United Kingdom, are a very rich and influential country. However, just yesterday the TV said that our economy is down on its knees, and the pound has lost its reigning power. Soon it will be overtaken not by the American dollar, but by the Euro.

All of this has happened thanks to some banks that lent money to people in America, who further learnt it to others as mortgages. It said most of the mortgage takers could not repay, and in due course, the Americans could not repay their British lenders, and that money was the pensions of our elderly people and our national savings.

This story does not add up for me. Does America have prisons? What do their prisoners actually do in their day-to-day time other than going to the gym and fighting amongst themselves? Are they also spoiled on tax payers' money, suing for silly damages, like my dad told me our prisoners are here?

Do Americans have children in care over there? And do they undergo various sufferings as we do here? This reminds me of a 2006 article I read on the internet the other night, the night I wept for ever having been born and ending up in care.

The newspapers quoted on the internet, if they are to be trusted, recently reported that there were 66,000 children in care. These children are more likely to end up unqualified, unemployed, homeless, or in prison than children brought up by biological parents. Many in care are, in effect, thrown out of the system at 17 and left to fend for themselves.

Children brought up by their parents on average stay at home until they are 24 and then move out gradually, with financial and emotional support continuing long after. Alan Johnson, the Education

Secretary, who narrowly avoided care at 12 when his mother died, said that children in care have been "failed by the system."

"The state needs to start acting like a traditional loving family," said Mr. Johnson. "It must raise its ambitions for these children and transform their life chances through better emotional, practical and financial support at home and in the classroom."

Some alleged independent report by the Centre for Policy Studies revealed where the 6,000 children who leave the £2 billion care system end up each year. A quarter of the girls are pregnant when they leave, and half become single mothers within two years. Half of prisoners under 25 have been through the care system and one-third of homeless were raised in care.

Ministers say that a lack of properly trained foster parents and staff in residential centres leads to difficult and often disturbed children being transferred between homes. Only five percent of foster parents have NVQ3 qualifications relevant to working with children. The experts further say that these foster parents often fail to support schooling as effectively as natural parents do.

In residential homes, 40 percent of managers lack relevant qualifications and only five percent of homes can show that 80 percent of the staff has the relevant NVQ3.

How can ill-trained staff, barely able to read and tick boxes, promote lifelong education for children? Is it the case of Israelites in Egypt being asked to make bricks without straw?

I have axes to grind with you, Mr. Chancellor.

Are you genuinely convinced that we children in care receive preparation adequate enough to enable us to practically survive in respectable professions upon leaving care?

A sizeable number—a quarter of all prisoners, as I understand—end up in prison. Are these really independent criminal activities, or are they activities well planned by smart individuals who notice that they, when innocent, receive far less attention and monetary support than their colleagues do in the "amusement parks," aka, prisons?

If you have settled on baiting all petty criminals to go behind bars, where they can wallow in milk and honey, how are you making these prisoners contribute back into the economy? If they do in some hidden ways, why are we still a struggling economy? Nonetheless, we manage to entertain prisoners in amusement park style and carry on funding unprovoked wars? The latest trend is to cut all spending to families, pensioners, and health and social services. What chance do we looked after children have of making it to innocent adulthood?

What products are made in prisons anyway? What percentage of GDP are these, if I may ask? Why can these vocationally experienced and seasoned ex-convicts not be swallowed into industries to obviate reoffending tendencies, considering they come with a ready, skilled, quality conscious contribution to society? Why does funding go to those most troublesome? Is rewarding people for being bad the new society plan?

Dina has three boys, each from a different father. From what she tells my mum, to whom she empties her heart's contents, none of the men was committed to stay. Dina herself is not willing to cling to any of them for fear of losing the council flat and single parent/children benefits. As it appears, with all the emotional, economic, and social struggles, two, if not all three, of the boys may end up in care, like their mother.

Did you read about Gary Greenhouse? Gary left care at the supposedly ripe age of 17. Given no prospects as a transitional adult, no serious career skills training, and no network to clinch him employment, Gary frequented the job centres. He went there so often that he knew most of the staff members by name. But having missed most of his schooling and without the foundation to justify his studying for his dream of being a barrister, frequenting the job centre was not enough to give him any job. Utmost, it provided him with paper evidence that he was actively looking for employment.

A teetotaller, it was not long before Gary gave in to the temptation of binge drinking. But he was too smart to be involved with rowdy groups. He made friends with most of the bouncers of clubs. But this meant that his money from the dole went straight to booze. Yet that was also Gary's downfall, at least in a short period of time.

He fell out with one of the bouncers, who had supplied him cocaine and weed as an initiation so that if he liked the experience he could begin selling it for the bouncer. Gary tried it, found it disgusting, and refused to pay. The bouncer threatened to bust him up, and Gary threatened him with unleashing his man-eating Doberman dogs onto his family and children, whom he claimed to know personally.

Apparently the bouncer became livid and apologised. But that was not the end of the story as the bouncer reported Gary to the police, alleging that he dealt in drugs and kept dangerous man-eating dogs.

Gary was picked up, and spent three days in the cooler while the police investigated the stories. Of course, they found Gary smelling skunk, but he explained the bouncer's offer. For lack of evidence, no charges were made and Gary was released.

By this time, Gary could not even pay the little he was supposed to contribute at the Assisted Housing Hostel. He was kicked out and became homeless. He was bereft of a roof and had not even a reputation to live up to.

That experience sobered him up. With the handouts from the dole, Gary racked his brains for ways to survive. He hid his miseries in a well cropped head and clean pressed clothes. In his own words, he was, "too proud to go back to social services."

A surprise even to himself, he still loved to frequent pubs and wish hours away on a bottle of Coke. Meanwhile, he developed a skill for observing people. He was able to sift them into groups of bored youths, disgruntled married adults, love-starved and attention-seeking women, and gold-digging starlets. There was yet an ill-defined group of young men and women. These seemed to spend more time socialising outside the pub than drinking and dancing inside.

Not knowing exactly what they sought, they never found it. Gary noticed one of those girls who seemed to only drink Coke, and he offered to buy her a drink. He followed her out and they sat on a free bench and talked at length.

Gary found himself opening up to this girl whom he barely knew. He mentioned his endless search for employment and asked her if she knew of any odd jobs that he could do while awaiting a better job. She asked him to phone her the next day.

They exchanged phone numbers. The following day, true as the rising of the sun, Gary phoned her. He realised that she was a mule. Using half of his dole money, he bought a few nodes and went off to see if he could pass them on for more mint. He did and made a hefty profit over time. After a few meetings with the girl, whose name turned out to be Zara, Gary realised that he could train more mules and make more money without him touching the stuff.

Gary realised there were a lot of Zaras out there, exploitable youth who were prepared to work. Youths no one wanted to give a job. He also realised that there was a substance to be traded, and people were willing to buy and use it.

He found a niche; he explored and exploited it. Zara linked him to PD, whatever his real name was, who linked him to tenant weed growers. They supplied Gary with year-round quantities from their greenhouse factories. Within a month, Gary left London and went to live in the outskirts, a train ride away, renting an entire flat to himself.

At twenty, Gary had stumbled onto a thriving market link, and he exploited it for a hefty sum. He kept clean hands, no sweat, and no involvement. He now drives a BMW. He runs his business through plenty of mules, with no strings attached.

The next time someone drives past you in a BMW with registration of something like GG1EFH, it will be Gary. We all call him "Gary Greenhouse." He has his motto: "Gary Greenhouse, Each for Himself" (GG1EFH).

Now that Gary went "greenhouse," who was he going to employ? Who would be the ultimate consumers of the weed? Who was he going to employ as his mules to peddle the drugs around? I am worried it could be my little sister, tempted by drug money.

Did I hear you say that you have children? Then be worried, be very worried, for they may unwittingly end up either as mules in search of a few pounds or destroy themselves consuming the weed from greenhouses. All because no respectable jobs were ever offered to the likes of Gary.

After reading this, would you still be looking for solutions to youth crime? Then, I am afraid I may still have more axes to grind with you, sir.

Latest from the news:

> *Cathy, formerly a looked after child, comes to a nasty end, buttered by a sugar daddy millionaire she tried to swindle.*

> *Mr. Johnson said that there would be a considerable "dead-weight cost" in paying the 37,000 foster parents for a role they do freely. But the move would "benefit the children," he said.*

> *"There is an 8,000 shortage of foster parents and very high turnover," he said. "If we professionalise their status, hopefully, there will not be this high turnover and the outcomes for the children will improve."*

Where is the good news, then, you may ask? Well, the media hasn't gotten it yet. If you do your homework on child placement correctly, once and for all, no child shall be shunted between placements. There shall be fewer Garys and fewer Zaras to be exploited.

As for me and my fellow children, all we really need is a guiding hand and loving and firm support to forge into a vocational career. Show us your boundaries, help us toe the line, and please do not force us out before we are ready.

Loads of love,

Taxie XXX

CHAPTER 14

Is My Road Home Safe, Mrs Queen?

Candle Mews,
Radnor-cliff Crescent
Folkestone,
CT20 2JQ

Today's date

Dear Mrs Anne Queen,

I would like to think that you have children of your own and that you can actively listen or empathise with me as a child. I wish I had sent you this letter in audio format because then you would get the messages in not just black and white, but in the untranslatable pain that comes in my quavering voice.

Today, I have been trying to examine my identity, to find my place in this wide world, if or whether I do have some future, where and how.

I would like to live with my parents. I would.

I really wish someone offered them help whenever they ran into trouble.

Yes I wish that part of this money that surfaces when there is a disaster, be it floods, terror scare, unsolicited wars, ever-expanding airports and runways, were made available to assist those members of the society who have it hard economically or who lack career training to employ themselves and make good working parents. Could that not have stopped masses from being on the dole, and from offloading or overloading their troubles onto us children till we end up in care?

How many children, now teens or adults, ever came out of care without scars, physical or psychological? Will those scars ever heal? Would it not be the best bate, or best investment, for the nation to invest in our well being right from home? Has the escalated assault, abuse, or neglect of children by their parents and relatives not been a cry for help as parents realise they cannot cope with their responsibilities in the current environment?

Who hears them? Get it from me, the insider: living in care is like living in prison (based on what my father has said about prison life). Even if you seem to be respectively well off, you share, empathise, and internalise the hurt, aches, and raw deal that your mates go through or have gone through. You begin to see life with a tainted view. When we children share stories about our broken backgrounds, we cannot help saying it as it was. Even if one may not be any more graphic than narrating, the wince of the eyes, the screwed face, as the pain or neglect is replayed in the eyes, punctuated by a checked sob, and clenched fists, says it all.

Mrs Queen, did you read about the suggestion that obese children should be taken into care? We got the story from the Metro Newspaper of 28 September, 2008, which James, one of the boys I share a house with, had picked up from the train station. What good would that do for these poor obese children?

Who in care homes has the emotional resilience and supply to meet the emotional needs that these children are currently receiving from their biological parents? How is taking a child into care for obesity solving the problem, if you even know what the problem is in the first place? How are you going to maintain the social bonds at their current strength between that child and the siblings and parents?

I have heard of a loving father whose pending divorce did his head in so much that he drowned himself and his beloved boy. This is the boy whose custody he feared of losing in the divorce. Does that not say everything about the depth of love and anguish a parent suffers through separation from his or her children?

Certainly, parents of such obese children would resent the society forever, and I would love to visit and talk to any parents that your ministry identified who overfeed their children to obesity on purpose. There are many glaring reasons that we poor children end up in care, and surely obesity should never be one of them.

No one likes to be called a "looked after child" or LAC. If you ask us, we shall tell you clearly: No one, not me, likes to be called a child in care. Social or institutional care is not necessarily a safe refuge, and given options, no child would ever end up in care. Neither should any child be used as a guinea pig for some social or psychological theory of some adult trying to score mercurial points.

Every child should be looked after by their biological parents, uncles, aunties, grannies, or in the extreme cases, should be adopted. No exceptions. And if you ever make exceptions, make them of exceptional quality.

We are in care, but we are not cared for. Materially, we might receive care, but emotionally and socially, we do not. We may have had poor food and seemingly inadequate clothing and lousy chores, but other than the extremes of physical and sexual abuse, we were loved and told off with love. We did not have to prove anything to be loved, nor did we ever have a feeling of being on the fringe of society.

Much as there is government support for the rehabilitation of drug addicts, could you not have used the money you spend on us and our carers to improve our parents' economic bases, employability, anger management, social commitment, self esteem issues, conflict resolution, and budgeting and shopping skills?

Hear it from us, the looked after children. We live being looked after. Our lives are empty and artificial as we are perpetually on the look-out for someone we can trust enough to feel the emptiness caused by our separation from our parents.

Yes, again, if we had it our own way, in our children's government, whose ministers would be all those who have undergone the anguish and have been assisted to come to terms and realise that their tormentors do not hold everlasting power over them. In such a kingdom, not one child should ever end up in any care home, not a children's home, nor a foster care. Adoption is as different as one gets from a new home and family for perpetuity.

Food alone is not our problem. Social frivolous security is. We children have to play and no outdoor life, when every possible open space is either private or possibly fenced or becomes a car park for some council or a shopping mall.

Public parks are riddled with the dangers of broken bottles, druggies' needles that no one is responsible to clear, and obscene messages. Even physical education in schools is over regulated as our tutors and teachers fear accidents and being sued.

If only you allowed us basic food and an active life and helped our parents to find honest jobs that enable them to look after us, our lives would not be ruined. Most tension in homes comes from parents being frustrated with their inability to afford a reasonably good life for themselves and their families.

My geography tutor showed me some interesting report from August 2008 by the World Health Organisation. It was initially interesting, but soon became worrying when I applied the facts to my own situation and those of other children in care.

Is it sobering to know that the poorest will die 30 years younger before the rich? It is sad that the average life expectancy in some poor parts of London is eight years lower than the Indian average. If it is true that children from Hampstead, North London, are likely to live 11 years longer than those from Kings Cross, is it biology or social injustice that shall kill off these children a decade sooner than others? I would like to believe that these details came from a normal population and not from studying children in care.

This is where I start being uncomfortable Mrs Queen. You are our health minister, or so I have heard. What chance do "looked after children" have of becoming respectable working and independent adults, to grow up, marry, and live in the likes of North London? I mean we, on average, cannot get a fair start in education, let alone proper career training.

Mrs Queen, listen to this. I went to see my old friends in Carshalton. To be honest, I have unusual friends in that they are either young men or very elderly women carers, with just a handful of girls my own age. Most of my friends in Carshalton have been in all sorts of gangs, dealt in skunk, snuffed, protect one another, and use guns just as teachers use pens.

We went out for a drink at some hideout where we usually go when we expect no nosy faces. In the course of the evening, somehow, our bunter moved on to our respective progress in life. I mentioned in passing that I was having extra tuition so that next year I could get good grades for my GCSE and go to university and become a medical doctor.

My friends laughed.

Tomtom—so nicknamed because he never ever gets lost—laughed so much that tears ran down his cheeks.

"What's wrong with you sister?" he asked, amid the laughter. "I thought you were smarter than that. You only have to study if you are not smart, unless you want to join those thieves in suits, also known as lawyers". Tomtom does not like lawyers at all ever since he saw a man he believed was clearly guilty be acquitted after being defended by a lawyer. "You just have to get rich or die trying, but school is unnecessary, as long as you know how to read and write." He shifted his weight onto the other foot as he wiped his mouth of spilt gin.

"Just get your brains together;" Geraldo added. "And plan big. If you pick your targets, pick them smarter than the airport muggers, those of the silly Securicor heist. There are bound to be casualties, but get what you want."

I became aghast as the meaning of what the boys had said sank in. I could not believe that Geraldo had just said that. "Are you out of your mind?" I retorted. "Why do it dirty and be on the run the rest of your life, when you can make it peacefully and enjoy your money?"

"Little sister," replied Geraldo, "stop fooling yourself. Look around you. How many of those who have degrees can afford a worry free holiday to Majorca or follow the year around sun in Bahamas? How many of those graduates have ever been given a free house, a tax payer funded car for free and around the clock, lifelong government protection?"

"Remember Ian Huntley and Maxine Carr, his girlfriend? After a brief stint in a cooler equipped with a state-of-the-art gym and a nutritionist calculated diet, what did the girlfriend get for her part in the crime? A new identity, an injunction stopping the media from even taking her photograph, a new house, and a supply of money to run her new life, and button press instant police protection. I bet you she has probably been trained to a top MI5 by now, rewarded for terminating the lives of those two innocent football lovers."

"Tell her, Brava,", piped Tomtom.

"Get real, little sister," Geraldo went on with new zest. "Every con in Belmash and elsewhere knows that even if you get a life pronounced in court, all you need to do is bow your head in seeming shame as you are led away. Once you're given your little dig and greeted by the ever-quizzical looks of the oldie pros in there, you just play it cool. By being obedient and seemingly helpful to the wardens without being seen to be betraying the inmates, you squeeze the years off. You are sure to be let out for good behaviour in less than a dozen years and given the definite rewards that even law-abiding citizens could not afford in twenty years."

"What?" I protested. "But that's plain wrong inn'it?"

"Call it what you will," went on Geraldo, as if ignoring my protest. "Peace of mind for you and your loved ones. Cynical as it may sound, little sister, but this is reality that defies common logic."

"You seem to be out of touch with reality, girl," teased Tomtom. "What parts of the country are you stashed in that keep you so blind? Remember St George School in West London? I shall remind you in case you have been away for a bit too long. You well and truly must have heard or read about Mr Philip Lawrence, the late headmaster, who in 1995 was stabbed to death by Learco Chindamo?"

I nodded, although I really had no idea who either of the two were and had never heard or read about them before that evening.

"Chindamo was," went on Tomtom, "this very year, given a new identity. New life, a new car, and moved to some secure secret location where he is freely housed, has a panic button for around the clock police protection, and a fat allowance to boot! Just after twelve years of steel pumping and profanity hearing, all of which you get used to behind bars. Note that even the asylum and immigration tribunal could not depot him to Italy lest they bleach his right to a family life."

Tomtom stressed "family life" with a sneer. He spoke with such knowing that I wondered when and where he learned all of this when he spent most of the time looking for weak spots to mash in and make quick money.

"It is a diabolical foolproof winner trick any clever fellow can use to tap the Queen's central bank and live on milk and honey all one's life." He quickly stuffed half a muffin in his mouth as he relished his tale. "Which clever con cannot use the trick successfully? It even worked for the pair who killed the poor boy James Patrick Bulger in Liverpool in 1993. One of whom is bragging behind bars about being bored in a private life. In the same system some convicts sue the government for thousands while others win millions of pounds on lotto and are allowed to keep their cash while still being fed from the taxpayers' pockets. Not even Disneyland can beat that winning formula!

"You just have to find one good thief out of those pin-stripe-suited greedy scoundrels whose offices dot the high streets. He will do all the talking for you while you are busy rowing in the gym.

"Their greed teaches them how to lie to win for you. They quote some quack imaginary rights, don't they? And you are protected and rewarded by the very justice system that sent you behind bars in the first place?" Tomtom patted Geraldo on the shoulder. "I think we need to keep this little sister informed."

"Certainly, Brava," replied Geraldo. "You see even Cain may have used the trick when he received protection from God almighty for having killed his own brother. You only have to play sorry and look like a convincingly changed person. And why not? If the game wins you a definite future in tranquillity, play it. Any sensible person would."

"Even the latest machine gunning technos shall get their share of early retirement pecks if they keep their wits about them." Tomtom passed me a miniature whisky and went on. "So tell me then, wise sister. Why study if for actually killing one soul, you can get in less than twelve years what educated ones fail to get in twenty years?"

I must have been stoned dead by the miniatures for with the exception of this chilling discussion, the rest of the details of the evening discussions faded out of my mind. This was one evening of confusion.

I had never been confronted by such contradictions among society in my life. The only ones I keep seeing are natural ones, such as why I had to be born in this particular family or in this particularly part of the world and end up in care. But I have come to terms with that. But the contradiction narrated by the boys takes the biscuit, Mrs Anne Queen,

It seems to be a well thought-out process whose decisions are made either by the likes of you or some robot-run courts. To be honest with you, this is the view discussed among my friends, who are members of various gangland kingdoms. Will they care about the value of the lives they take in the process of meeting their greed?

I know I am protected by having friends in these scary places and dangerous groups. If I were to be killed, my mates would avenge my death. But saying that, I could be targeted for exactly the same reasons: having friends in the wrong kingdom or belonging to the wrong postcode. So I cannot really guarantee being alive in the next five years, in this con-protecting society, can I Mrs Queen? I mean, if people are rewarded with more protection and money (spent on them) for killing others, while the dying and bereaved are stuffed with hollow memories and emptiness.

In childhood, you can be rewarded for sulking. For throwing tantrums you receive attention, which soon good parents frowned upon and ignored. Now if in teen to adulthood you are paid and protected for being violent and killing others, what is your message to us as we grow in this economically difficult society?

I now have to rethink my priorities and all the messages teachers have been pumping at us. Did those teachers miss the obvious and is that the reason why the average teacher cannot afford a decent holiday in the Seychelles?

Do I still follow my doctor dream that may take at least ten years before I can become a general practitioner, and yet have no guarantee that I shall make it?

Otherwise, where are the educated idols and heroes? How come they do not seem to walk the common streets or visit the likes of those of us living in care homes? If they exist, do they know there are children in care who are searching for someone to look up to?

You never read about such people in the newspapers, nor do we hear of them compared to reports about violence and crime on the TV. I have heard about Allan Sugar, or Sir, as I hear he is called, about Bill Gates, Donald Trump, and Oprah Winfrey. I hear they are filthy rich, but I have never heard how their education, if any, built them a foundation to the top. At least none of my teachers could ever give me a true example when we asked if one of them could be invited to speak and give us inspiration. What are we poor and discriminated kids to do when the examples of daily life are mostly negative reports in the news?

Did you ministers and justice people forget that even kids watch television and read the newspapers, even if only sporadically? We discuss such issues amid all the play and backbiting. How then should those children with troubled backgrounds go any other way? Which way, then, when this is the bizarrely exciting yet publicly rewarding path, that enables you to clean your tracks with a new identity? When after your crimes accounted for, reasoned, and excused, you continue on another page?

I understand that if I succeed and get a job, part of my taxes shall be used to maintain the chosen lifestyles of the like of Chindamo, Venables, and the so-called Crookhand. If they are prized for being evil, and I am taxed for abiding by the law, is there any point in being honest and hard working?

The boys talked about Brendan Harris who was associated with the death of Ryan Herbert, and the estimated costs of maintaining the new identity lifestyles of ex-cons. They left it to my imagination to guess how much money is being spent on such ex-cons, respectively, when you add up their planned luxury and the protection.

To show me just the tip of the iceberg, Nosy Neil, who rarely speaks in a group, said he would show me a newspaper cutting he had obtained from the Guardian. To my horror, the Guardian reported that the 100,000 of public money used on the injunctions hearing alone, not including protection, would have paid for 108 cataract operations, 23 hip replacements, 20 knee operations, or 16 heart bypass grafts. Or they could pay the wages of nine hospital cleaners that could save millions of lives from dying of C Difficile in the government's filthy hospitals.

If such is the grandiose amount of money spent on one crime tainted individual, I think I am getting the message. Could the boys have had a point then, when they said that this was the latest gold dust trophy hunting? In other words, a new way of becoming a silent Lewis Hamilton, a new Beckham, with all expenses paid for?

Is it true that this is tax payers' money, money that I know is deducted from every honest working individual, even when my dad could not save enough to buy me the fashion handbag of the day? Even now, my mum cannot get all the money she wishes she had to train as a lawyer and rebuild her drug ravaged life.

We children in care do think, and we are affected by what is going on around us and what we see on the news. What no one can predict is what we make of the messages you flash at us. Where do you inspire us to go? We are not exactly like children in family homes with their biological parents, fighting and yet ticking the calendars for the next birthday.

At times, we feel like we are on the fringe of society. We may not cry often in public, but we certainly do in the privacy of our bedrooms. We identify more with those behind bars than the rest of you in posh cars.

What is justice, madam minister, and where is the security for the health of the average person?

For now, I fear for my family because of the "kill and get rewarded" culture that our justice system grooms.

You just have to be in the wrong place at the wrong time, and like the poor Rhys, you will be killed. In the same breath, the killers are on the queue to be rewarded with fully comprehensive insurance of economic and social security for half a dozen years ahead. I surely do not think it is fair to be poorly rewarded or even ignored in society for being uneventfully honest.

Which way do I go with my life Mrs Queen? With killers being rewarded, can my sister safely walk home from school in the evening? Which youth know they shall live past their next birthday?

Mrs Queen, do you truly exist as I do? If yes, then I would be very grateful, Mrs Queen, if you spared some minutes to clear my confusion. If you could visit some of us children in care, if you revealed any support we can have to see us back into the normal society, you could help us wash off our stigma and the yoke society has put on us.

Mrs Queen, this is what I had kept for you, a special version of my thoughts from the day. I dared to dream and share with the privileged you. Could it be that your options are being reorganised, and you will be restoring the people's faith in your team? Or will you let us children be informed by the likes of my gangland friends? Maybe you simply have to show us who the effective leaders are—the ministers or the crook crew?

Lots of tender love from singing winds of Folkestone, the raging waves of Hythe, and the white cliffs of Dover,

Taxie XXX

CHAPTER 15

Shall We Apologise to Mrs Skinner?

Candle Mews,
Radnor-cliff crescent
Folkestone,
CT20 2JQ

Today's date

One kind word can warm three winter months. —Japanese proverb.

Dear Teachers,

This letter is for one teacher in particular: Mrs Kitty Skinner, who at one point served as a head teacher for a seaside school.

I am writing to offer apologies to Mrs Kitty Skinner, the onetime head of St Nunes Secondary School, now the Dash Academy. You may remember that two years ago there was mayhem at your school over Easter holiday. Two innocent girls were punished for it, and a janitor, Mr Mink, was fired. A week later, the carpet in your office stunk to heaven and you had to replace it. Do you really want to know what happened?

I shall tell you the story. How do I know it? Well, I was on a tour of the seaside town that day and happen to have heard it straight from the horse's mouth.

On this day, two classes were vandalised, windows were smashed, window latches were unscrewed, and one room, ,maybe your office, had a puddle of water on the carpet, or so you believed. It was code named *Fiat Cinque* as it only took five minutes. Let it last five minutes. No more than five minutes. The trashing operation lasted five minutes or less.

The two girls were Tanya and Monica. Tanya was a tall, plump Latina with long, shiny black locks that accepted great styles of curls and waviness, often falling down beyond her shoulders. She had brushed her bangs to the side, making them flow well with the rest of the wavy layers.

She had it parted slightly off centre with different amounts of curls through each layer. Oval faced, Tanya's long waves and curls gave her great looks that attracted lots of winks and whistles. She had long eyelashes, large brown eyes, and thick round lips. Her massive structure and heavily laden chest were accentuated by a generous behind to which J Low would shy away by miles. In shops, she passed for 21 and bought fags with no questions asked.

Monica was an equally tall blonde, witty and chatty as tradition goes, but certainly not dumb. She was particularly outstanding for her long legs, a very flat midriff, and she mostly wore tight Levi jeans. She wore expensive cologne as a signature.

Being square faced, Monica always had her hair cut to a fringe that made her face look like an arch. Whenever she let her well nourished hair down, one barely saw her ears. Only the 'hula-hoop' earrings showed that she had ears at all.

The girls were out for fun and excitement on a cold February evening. For one, it was a day of innocent exploration. For the other, it was a mission of vengeance. The school was trashed on Tuesday, but the story started on Friday.

It was a typical front cover story, one some news reporter would have had a party to cover. I had just returned from visiting my mum and a little sister in Newham in London over the Easter weekend. I had a good time, lots of laughing with my mum and little sister, as we had a picnic in the Battersea Park.

You see, for a long time, I had never really been happy with my mum. After her going behind my dad's back and having him swindled by her boy toy, I did not see my dad again. I blame mum squarely for that. One day, her boy toy had been making funny faces at me and invading my space. I felt uncomfortable and told my mum about him the following evening, but she did not think much about it.

When Mum and my little sister went to the co-op for some groceries, she left me lying on my bed reading. Billy, the boy toy, came up and asked me why I had told lies to my mum about him.

"What lies?" I asked, looking up at him puzzled.

"You smile and wink at me and tell your mum that I wanted to assault you?"

He did not give me a second to respond. Barely finishing his sentence, he pretended to stumble and fell over me, on the bed, pinning me face up. He held one hand over my mouth.

He was so quick, brutal, and strong that before I got over the shock of him falling onto me, he had pulled my track suit bottoms and pants away. All the while he kept his hand on my mouth and shouted at me not to struggle. I had not known we were living with a monster.

I started crying as he got off me. It was so painful that I cried continuously. I spat at him, called him "swine," and got under the duvet to hide. Of course this was too late; I had already been damaged.

I do not really know what he told my mum when she came back from shopping. She stormed up into my room and called me a mean slut. "How dare you call your mum's boyfriend to your bed?"

She gave me two quick burning slaps and stormed back downstairs. You see, my mum is a failed fitness instructor and a former student of kick boxing. So I knew better than to retaliate, no matter how badly I wanted to do so.

I knew that when she spoke in a particular tone, she would not listen to anything I could say. Indeed, loving eyes can never see, as demonstrated by my mum, and possibly many mothers of some unlucky girls that are abused and are not believed.

I had heard about girls being raped but had never thought it could happen to me. I did not want my little sister to know, and yet I wondered if I could easily walk properly without her suspecting. Would anyone believe me? Why had Mum gone to the shop if she knew her boyfriend was coming over?

Now my mum had quickly believed him and reacted by blaming me without giving me a second to explain. Her anger made her an accomplice in my mind. I curled up into a ball in my bed and sobbed endlessly. Deep down, I really wanted to poison her and her paedophile boyfriend. How dare she believe that I had an eye for her weed-stinking boyfriend? Not long thereafter, I hardly spent a night at my mum's place even when visiting from my residential home.

My mum had actually not believed that I had been raped. That evening, while still bearing the pain, I went and tried to tell Debbie, my mum's friend. She immediately phoned my mum, who told her that I had just made it up.

I told Debbie that I would poison both my mum and her boyfriend, for what he had done to me. I actually meant it and was already thinking of all the poisonous substances we had for cleaning the bathroom.

My sister and I were also being starved. When mum actually had money, she was spending it on cocaine. Her defence of her toyboy was the last straw. After she allowed him to accuse me—a girl of twelve—of flirting with him, I wanted nothing to do with her for as long as she was seeing the scoundrel. I was still hurting inside.

I refused to go back home. Considering that at the time we were literally struggling with basic meals, I realised I had reached my limit. Debbie called the police, who came with social workers. I refused to go through any public questioning and so Billy was briefly detained and released. Social services immediately placed me under a supervision order. That marked the beginning of my life in care.

Having gone into care, I kept reflecting over what had happened to me. I contacted my social worker and insisted that both Billy and my mum should be arrested for hurting me. Strangely, my social worker at the time avoided dealing with the issue head on and told me to let sleeping dogs lie.

Three years on, and my mum broke away from Billy and came in tears apologising for not believing me. She only opened her eyes when Billy was caught and arrested for abusing Stella, our neighbour's nine-year-old daughter. He had lured her with sweets and a fiver.

Thank God I never caught any nasty infection or anything like that. But six months later, I had to have a small operation as I leaked wee each time I tried running, and I always experiencing some burning each time I wanted to pee. I told my carer that my body had been damaged by Billy, my mum's boyfriend.

My carer contacted the police again, and Billy admitted it and had his sentence extended. I hope that he is not allowed out ever again.

Anyway, my relationship with Mum improved a little bit after I went into care. This time, when I came visiting Mum for a weekend, we had a lovely time together. While I have forgiven her for choosing the abusive boyfriend over me, I still find her substandard with discipline. Probably trying to make up for her mistake, she will now let me and my sister get away with unacceptable behaviours.

Too often, I secretly cry for my dad who had no nonsense with discipline. He would immediately give you a stinging slap if he told you off about something and you ignored him. Yet he was full of loving hugs, hugs that I have missed for nearly two years.

After the picnic in the park, I went out to King Edward Pub with the "Hamlet Crew," as my new group of friends called themselves. They filled me in with the latest gossip: who had died, who had moved, who had gone in the cooler, and the latest equipment and mobile phones in use. We drank a lot and got stoned on weed and skunk. There I was again, pushing boundaries with my mum as my dad would not have tolerated.

I went home half dazed. But then Richard always looked out for me and drove me home. He always said that I talked and walked like his little sister, and he treated me as he would treat her.

You see, I had known most of the group members from as far back as age seven, at Green Acre primary school. While others had moved away, when parents changed jobs or retired, those who stayed always kept in touch. We shared food and drinks, joys and frustration, and often partied on chicken from KFC.

As soon as I got home, I asked my little sister to run me a hot bath. However, I nearly drowned when I fell asleep in the bath. Vicky, my little sister, had to fish me out, almost pulling me out by my hair. With only a towel around my waist, I hobbled into bed.

I could not even remember dreaming at all. I awoke with a throbbing headache on Sunday and could not believe that it was past midday. My body just refused to get up though.

Mummy had brunch waiting, but I hardly enjoyed it, as I rushed around looking for my books to do homework for Monday. You see, I am not that bad at studying. I had requested an additional lesson from my private tutor over the Easter holidays. All went well up to Thursday, and I was in great learning mood.

For once, I just whizzed over the notorious algebra equations. I was let out early on Friday, having agreed with my tutor that I would do my homework at Mum's over the weekend, ready for Monday morning. So I had faithfully brought my books with me all the way from Folkestone.

I needed to at least have started it, to find some excuse that I had got stuck. Yet I also needed to say a quick hello to the Hamlet crew. I needed to let them know that I was okay and to thank them for having looked after me at the "KG," as we fondly called the King George Pub. Soon, it would be three and then the taxi would be waiting outside to drive me back to Kent.

You know, this is the part I both liked and loathed about being in care. Each time I came to visit Mum, social services would send me a taxi all the way from London to Folkestone. On return, the same taxi would be at outside the door at the time that I said I wanted to leave. My home manager made sure I had a weekend allowance to spend at my mum's. Similarly, if Mum wanted to come down and visit me, she was brought down by a taxi and taken back to London by a taxi.

At times, I wondered how such generosity would abruptly disappear on leaving care, as Titus and Gary had told me. Anyway, that is a different matter to await me another year or so. For now, there was this homework to be started and hellos to be said to the crew. Come three o'clock there would be dirty clothes to be collected from around the room and the laundry downstairs and packed ready for the taxi to Kent.

As agreed, the taxi showed up by half-past five in the afternoon. I slept for most of the way. We reached Candle Mews, Folkestone around half-past seven in the evening of that Sunday. I was still dazed and pretended to be tired each time the driver asked me why I looked sleepy. I lied that I had hardly slept, having spent the previous night dancing and drinking at my cousin's party.

He simply accepted my explanation. Or he knew better than to quiz me over my private social life. The reality was that I was in a full hangover, dry mouthed and always gulping water. These are the effects of mixing beer, spirits, and spliff.

Needless to say that I dreaded Monday, as I had not scribbled even a line of my homework. I would have to disappoint my tutor. You see, he is one in a million. I knew immediately when I saw him that he understood. He was the male version of Angella, my former carer at a previous home.

He knew too much about me and I could not help but open myself up to him. He could easily have been my dad. He was, however, very much in touch with the youthful side of his past. If I was upset with something and looked like I wanted to cry, before starting or midway in his lesson, he would ask me to go to my room and calm down.

He even offered to listen to me if I wanted to talk about it. I needed a listening ear, and listen he would. I told him all the nasty things that had happened in my life and how even people that were closest to me had misunderstood me.

He was very sympathetic and always reminded me that other people had their own weaknesses, including betrayal. He said that I needed to look after number one: myself, much as I wished others were true to me. I needed to just consider them as possible helpers in my life, but people are individuals and do not necessarily owe me anything. Such a message sounded outrageous at first. But the more he repeated it, the more sense it started making. I soon learned that others' behaviours were not worth my grief.

Surprisingly, despite knowing so much of my personal weaknesses, my tutor still thought the world of me. No teacher had treated me like that before. He encouraged me so much that I learned millions of things from him, beyond the class work.

For example, I would be surprised if you, Mrs Kitty Skinner, know the necessity of having at least two toothbrushes in use at any one time.

Yes, it is necessary. This gives one toothbrush a chance to dry up and cut the build up of germs that accumulate from being damp under everyday use. He taught me small but useful tips like that.

He always taught in such a relaxed mood and with such freedom that I still felt guilty about not working hard on my homework after the lessons. Each time I needed a fag break, he let me have it, so long as we made it up later. Sometimes, he went to see some of my teachers to find out exactly what I had covered with them. On those few visits to my conventional school for consultation, every teacher he talked to went ruptured with attention. He was always there for me, despite seeing me only on Mondays and Wednesdays.

Now you can understand why I dreaded meeting him on Monday without any finished homework. Too stoned to think straight, what was a girl to do? I worried and worried and tried to look through my work and see what I could quickly write up.

But, thundering typhoons and rotten raspberries! The worst had already happened. I had forgotten my books including the assignment diary at my mum's!

"Oh, sugar," I said to myself. I had promised my tutor that I would be particularly good this time. I couldn't believe I had done the exact opposite. I had let him down and let myself down. I cried myself to sleep.

It was already Monday morning when I opened my eyes to the sound of some persistent bird that still sang to dawn even though winter was not really gone. It was well past dawn. Half-past eight still felt like one o'clock in the morning. I just wanted to sleep.

I opened the curtains and lay back on the bed, looking outside the window. The still rather distant April sun filtered through the lace curtain over the sash windows. Then Gringo, the albino squirrel, was perched on the cherry tree branches that kissed the window ledge. I quickly got up, put on my gown, half waving to Gringo outside the window. I went to the bathroom and proceeded downstairs.

Knowing that Gringo was lonely, I had a quick bath, rinsed my mouth with mint, quickly dressed, and went out to give her some bread crumbs. By the time I returned upstairs to do my hair, it was already coming to nine o'clock, and anytime now my tutor would be knocking on the door.

I quickly tiptoed to the office downstairs, but there was only Irma, the day carer. I greeted her in the most ill sounding voice I could muster. I told her that I felt unwell. "I feel soooo ill, Irma," I said, dragging the words. "I am afraid; I won't be able to attend the lessons this morning."

"Oooh, you poor thing," Irma responded. "But is it not too late now to inform, Mr Thomas? He may actually be knocking on the door any moment now."

"I am sorry, I even woke up late," I maintained. "Anyway, I shall apologise to him in person as well."

Irma called the tutor on his mobile and awkwardly apologised on my behalf. She later told me that he was actually on the corner turning onto our road. As it was, he had to go back. I hated myself for putting him through that waste of time. Mr Thomas did not deserve those lies.

I also phoned him and apologised repeatedly while deliberately coughing into the receiver to make him realise I was feeling real bad. I said that I would certainly have his homework ready by Thursday. I was actually hinting to him that I was most likely not going to be attending the lessons the next day either.

He was not so easily shaken off. He said he would phone Candle Mews later in the day to see how I was getting on.

No sooner had he left than I made myself a strong black coffee, rolled a fag, and took some more bread crumbs to feed Gringo in the garden. I fed Gringo, finished the fag and downed the coffee, but still felt rotten. I remembered that Gary had bought me six miniature whiskies the previous Saturday, and I still had three in my handbag.

I drank one and felt a lot better. My head cleared and I also remembered that I had not seen Laura since Wednesday of the previous week. Laura, a tall stocky girl who looked like a bouncer, was my friend from Deanmill House in Hythe.

Unlike me, Laura, my best friend in the area, was only thirteen and went to Brain Beach, the four classed school that Crystal Care runs for children in its residential homes. This covered key stage one onto the earlier part of key stage three. But for GCSE, one went to either Brockenpost, the nearest mixed secondary school, or the home hired private tutors for you. I was in the latter category.

By midday, I told Irma that I felt a bit better and wanted to go and see Laura, while having fresh air. I also requested to be allowed to stay a bit longer so that I could meet Mrs Green, Laura's home tutor, to ask for some guidance on my outstanding piece of homework.

I phoned Laura, who as usual had a long day plan. We were going to hit town and indeed hit the seaside. "What seaside?" I hear you asking. Folkestone is not seriously considered a seaside. Ramsgate was the real seaside for us, as it had loads of little hideouts from which we could sip cold Coke and enjoy seeing distant boats. You bet the mysterious white cliffs of Dover were en route!

When I told Laura about the two remaining bottles of miniature whiskey from the weekend, she said that it would be nice to drink them at the pier with our feet soaking in cold water. That sounded cool.

I put on my make-up, a tight pair of jeans that accentuated my figure, a low cut top, and tied my hair in a ponytail. I took my handbag and rushed to meet Laura at the bus station. We bought gold rider tickets that would take us to Canterbury, Whitstable, Herne Bay, Margate, Ramsgate, Dover, and back to Folkestone.

Laura reached the bus station a bit late, saying that she had stopped over at Sainsbury's, buying a few more drinks and snacks. She had the most unusual make up for a simple day out. It was as if she was getting ready for a night out.

"You must be mad, Laura," I said to her. "Is there something I need to know? Look at you!" She had diamond studded earrings and was basically dressed to kill. Or better said, dressed for the night, leaving little to the imagination.

"Wait till we reach Ramsgate," she replied.

"What? What are we doing in Ramsgate?"

"Keep your questions," she replied coolly, while passing me a packet of ready salted crisps and opening one for herself.

We got onto the Canterbury bus, shared a seat, and also shared Laura's headphones, listening to the Sugar Babes on her MP3 all the way to Canterbury. Then we changed buses for Herne Bay. It was when we reached the bus station in Westgate, Margate that I realised that we had not agreed how and where we would be spending the time here.

I was hoping we would go down to the beach in Westgate, get some ice cream at the pavilion and enjoy it while splashing our legs in the water at the pier or while lying down on our towels on the beach. I then thought that we would spend most of the afternoon at the pavilion, then the Winter Gardens, and go window shopping in Margate high street leading on to Clifton Ville.

But Laura had other ideas.

We quickly went down to the pavilion but hardly bought anything. We each bought an ice cream at a café and briskly walked on to the train station. "Wait here," she had said handing me her part of the speakers and the MP3. She then went for the ladies' toilets.

I sat on the bench listening to more music and half wondering how I was going to lie to Irma about my assignment. While I was lost in my daydreaming, ten minutes later a hand tapped me on my shoulder. It was a young woman of seemingly Indian background with the bindi (traditional red spot) midway between her eyes and loosely flowing but smooth hair that was plaited into a rope and went down her back onto her waist.

I nearly jumped out of my skin before realising that it was Laura when she smiled. This side of Laura, changing appearances, I had not known. We headed for the town centre and did window shopping in the high street.

We looked at a few clothes shops and left. We ate more crisps as we headed for the bus station again. This time for Ramsgate. Curiosity took the better of me.

"To be honest, Laura," I started. "I am becoming hungry and at the same time anxious. What exactly are we seeing in Ramsgate?"

"My boyfriend," Laura replied without batting an eyelid. I broke down laughing. That was the biggest joke of the day! Laura did not exactly dislike boys, but she enjoyed flirting with them and then putting them off by claiming that she was gay!

As soon as we reached the Ramsgate bus station, we dropped off and decided to walk into the town centre. The road that we took passed by St Nunes Secondary school, which was obviously shut for the Easter holidays. It was around 5:45 in the evening and there appeared to be no one at the school except the janitor who was at the gate.

"Hi Dennis," Laura said to the janitor.

"Do you know him?" I asked, surprised.

"He is the janitor here by day," Laura went on, "and the bouncer at the Cliff View Pub in Dover by night."

It was then that I saw the two girls, Tanya and Monica. Tanya knocked excitedly at the gate, which the Janitor opened before he even asked what the girls were after.

"Hallo, Mr Mink," Tanya piped confidently walking in and giving him a bear hug.

The janitor hesitated briefly before recollecting himself. Everyone could have seen that he had been thrown off his emotional balance. "Oh Hallow err, remind me your name please."

"Tanya. Remember me at the Cliff View last Wednesday, Mr Mink?"

"Of course, anyway, call me Dennis," the janitor offered. "So what goodies did you bring me then?" he further asked suggestively.

"Well, for starters, this here is my friend Monica. Monica, my friend Dennis," said Tanya turning to the janitor again. "He looks after me very well at the Cliff View in Dover."

"Of course, Tanya. Glad to meet you, Mr Mink, eerr Dennis." Monica seemed to blush a bit. "Tanya has been talking about you."

"Oh really, I hope it was something good." The janitor took his jumper off and pulled two chairs for the girls to sit down.

"What have you had for lunch then?" Tanya inquired settling herself in a tiny chair. She deliberately started fiddling with her jacket, revealing more of her cleavage. "Oh, I need to shed some more weight; I am already feeling warm from this little walk."

The fiddling captivated the janitor's attention and Tanya moved her chair closer. Opening her bag, she offered him a quarter pounder from McDonald's.

"Oh, perfect," said the janitor warming up even further. "Just what I needed, you know. All I had was black coffee after black coffee, all day."

"Well enjoy it then," Tanya replied. "You won't guess this." Tanya shot her hand into her handbag. "Something to wash the burger down with?" she went on, taking out some three cans of beer and a bottle of gin. She turned to Monica and said, "Where are those minnies?"

"Ooh little darlings, what are you doing to me? Spoiling me rotten or trying to make me lose my job?" he joked.

"You started it last Wednesday," Tanya replied. "A good turn deserves another, remember?"

They shared a can of beer each, opened the gin, and halfway, Tanya took the bottle of gin, which by now was half gone, and put it under her chair.

"What are you doooing?" protested the janitor, trying to reach for the bottle. "That was one of the smoothest gins I have had for ages."

"Here now, and don't choke yourself," said Tanya giving him the Laphroaig Quarter Cask Miniature. It was a single 5cl/55.7% distillery bottling. One of those pretty little minis with a powerful punch. One of the most explosive ones.

"These are the remainders from my cousin's birthday bash of last Saturday," Tanya said, giving the janitor another bottle of the miniatures. "You obviously could not have drunk while minding the door."

The janitor's eyes lit up. He was enjoying himself with the girls. Tanya stood up, took her handbag, and excused herself. "Mind the bottle of gin, Dennis," she said. "Don't let Monica finish it off before

I come. Now Dennis, which loo is clean enough for this princess to use?"

"Oh Tanya, use the staff one. The staff room is just after the second door to the right of the reception. You still remember your way around here don't you? It wasn't long when you were a student." The janitor reached over for the remaining gin, downed it with Monica giving no protest.

"No Dennis," Tanya replied. "But that gin did not help me. Besides, can I remember the door combination? They keep changing them, you know."

"Ooh, C2005 hash, girl. Now get going before you pop a stinker for us!" the janitor said, waving Tanya away.

"Fiat cinque!" Monica said shouting the operation length code reminder after Tanya. "Cinque, remember!"

"Excuse me," asked the janitor puzzled. "What did you say?"

"Never mind," replied Monica. "It is our joke about the little fiat car Tanya hopes to buy. I tease her that she needs to shed more weight, otherwise she shall not fit in it."

"Oh, stop it," the janitor protested. "She is not that bad you know. Good curves in the right places: J Low style bum and all the goodies, uuhmm. Cor blimey guv! What more can a man ask for?" The janitor mused, much to himself.

Near the staff room, Tanya looked at the combination lock and then changed her mind. She went round the block. At the back of the staff room, she identified a tap of water, which was at the foot of the window to the head teacher's office. She got a double pair of latex gloves and two clean kitchen towels out of her bag. She put the gloves on and wet the two towels. She looked around and saw some bricks near the flower beds. Wrapping two bricks in the wet towels, she stood directly on the window ledge and using her brick loaf hit it with her two hands.

It was a trick Tanya had learned from her demolition uncle. The window shattered silently inwards, with the shards hardly flying about. She did it again and again leaving a wide gaping hole. She stood back and admired her achievement.

She unwrapped the bricks and carefully replaced them.

She looked around and said to herself, "We don't want any innocent students getting hurt on these." She picked up any outstanding pieces of glass and carefully wrapped them in the wet towels. She put the folded towels in a plastic bag and returned them to her handbag.

Tanya inspected her hands and assured that she did not have any scratches. She carefully walked back to the front of the staff room. She had peeled one set of gloves and put them in the bag and was left with the lower set that was dry. With these on, she worked the combination keys, went into the staff room toilet, and unrolled a toilet roll. She socked the various pieces and walked across to the door that led to the head teacher's office from the staff room.

She tried the combination lock, but it would not open. Racking her brains, she realised that the figures combined into a year. "Green heads," she thought. "This must be child's play." She tried the same figures in reverse, but the door wouldn't open. She then tried replacing one end digit, then hash. The door obliged.

Tanya quickly looked around the room. Broken shards of glass littered the other side of the desk. She moved the chair over and found the diary on top of the in tray. She opened a number of pages with dates of the coming week. She then inserted the wet tissue bits as page markers. She picked a stick of glue from the nearby tray and glued the pages together. "That's your greetings," she mumbled to herself. She then quickly looked at the walls and saw the clock. Cinque. A minute and half to go.

Moving to the corner of the desk, she moved a carton of new books aside, left some wet mystery on the carpet for "Kitty the Callous." She then thought, "Is it enough? Should I or should I not?" were her thoughts. But the liquor propelled her judgement otherwise and Tanya moved the books carton back, saw a kitchen paper roll, and took some, making a two layered napkin. Laying it down carefully directly behind the head's chair she used more paper glue. Tanya left another mystery on the chair, leaving the room with some unusual fragrance.

She quickly dashed to the mirror in the ladies' room and adjusted her attire and her hair and looked at the wall clock. Cinque. Barely fifteen seconds left.

She quickly shut the door behind her, went across the staff room, and shut the other one. She walked over to the tap nearest to the porter's lodge where Monica and the janitor were still chatting away.

"I am getting thirsty already," she said attracting the others' attention. "I hope my gin is still there, Dennis?"

"Too late mate," the janitor mumbled, barely audible. Having combined the gin and the 55.7 percent miniatures, his eyes could hardly stay open.

"You have nearly killed me girls," he said. "Mind if I shut my eyes for a bit?"

"Not at all, guv," said Tanya. "But me and Monica shall quickly run into town and get some fish and chips. So you better come and shut this gate for now, then you can have a proper rest."

The girls picked up their bags, the now empty cans, bottles, and the burger container, and left. The janitor struggled to his feet, shut the gate, and settled back, pulling his chair against the wall and his hood over his face.

Tanya and Monica then quickly disappeared into the next street. Rushing to the nearest KFC, they went into the ladies toilet.

"Time to go mate," Laura said to me, jostling me out of my momentary shock and daydream.

We had been lying on the beach park for nearly an hour. Two looked-after-children from two children's residential care homes. Laura had taken off her Indian wig and mask and with it the bindi. She had also shed her oval face and the subsequent Latina look she had assumed.

We walked to the bus station, boarded the bus, and headed home.

"What was all that about then?" I asked Laura before we reached her house.

It was another hour before Laura finished the details, at the end of which I felt less guilty. I rung my house and told Irma that I had a migraine but was feeling better and would soon be home.

Have you got it yet Mrs Kitty Skinner?

I am writing this letter of apology not because of you, but because in repairing the window pane and replacing the carpet in your office, you used school funds. I wish there was a way of charging you personally for the damages.

So I am really sorry for the impact what we made, or specifically that Tanya made, robbing some students of amenities the money could have bought.

In case you are not so smart, let me spell it out for you: Tanya is Laura and Monica is me and below is the entire story.

Four years ago, you had a year eight student who came to you on transfer from the London area. She was a looked after child who had lost a lot of schooling in between. However, she was far from dull. With the help of a tutor, she did a lot of reading to catch up with what she had missed. When her placement broken down, she moved homes frequently. Her new residential home was near you, hence her coming to your school.

You obviously knew that she was a looked after child from a children's home. She was very nervous and insecure, but she put up a front which you interpreted as arrogance or being a loner. Fellow year eight students showed interest in helping her and invited her to join them. One of those was Mandy, a girl of Asian background, whose mother, herself Asian but married to an English man, was an English teacher in the school.

Little did the new girl, Zena was her name, realise that her class was divided into pecking order feuds. I bet that even you, Mrs Kitty Skinner, may never have known this.

Because Zena put up a fighting front to protect her inner insecurity, other students who felt they were the rulers of the class wanted her in their group. Just before break time, they invited her to go with them. Zena declined, choosing to go with the more modest group with Mandy instead.

During lessons, when Zena had excused herself to go to the toilet, one of the militant girls quickly excused herself and followed Zena. She demanded to borrow Zena's Chanel perfume, which Zena declined. She then told Zena that she had to join her and her mates or she would have a tough time in the school. Zena returned to class, and Yatola, for that was her name, followed her back into class.

Being a looked after child, Zena knew that the general expectation from authorities was not brilliant. So she kept a low profile. On her way home, she phoned Mandy, her new friend, and told her what Yatola, the militant, had said to her.

This went on for three days during Zena's first week in your school, and each time something happened, Zena confided in Mandy. The following week, Mandy told her mum about what was going on. Mandy's mum confronted Yatola, who denied everything.

During lunch hour, Yatola and her three friends had followed Zena and Mandy who were lying on the grass in the playground. They deliberately started harassing them and calling Mandy racially abusive names, saying she was a dimwit refugee who had only gotten a place in your school because her mother taught there. They told Zena that unless she joined them, the masters would give her silent punishment to which the teachers would have no evidence to believe her.

At that point, Zena stood up for herself and told the group that she was a girl from the London area and knew how to look after herself should they try any tricks. Then, one of the girls swore and spat at her. Zena spat back.

The girls retreated and quickly reported to the class teacher that Zena had been picking fights. They alleged that she and Mandy had spat on them.

The class teacher called the two innocent girls and Yatola was already waiting for them. Yatola then went on with her obviously rehearsed yarn that was miles from the original by now.

Each time Mandy or Zena tried to speak, the class tutor shushed them down. She then gave them a long dressing down.

Having listened for some time, Zena responded. "You haven't even heard our side of the story. That's unfair."

"You should know better than to backchat," she told Zena. "Now both of you, off to the head teacher's office now!"

Zena and Mandy were frog matched to your office. You were already in a bad mood, probably due to something domestic or God knows what.

As soon as you listened to the class teacher, you told the girls, "Both of you are suspended till further investigation. As for you. Zena, you can never come back, as I shall not allow you to poison my well-behaved girls with your shameful street habits."

It later developed that you threatened to sack Mandy's mum for siding with Zena and confronting Yatola. Mandy's mum was still serving probation, and she had been newly married.

You did not consider how many things could be messed up because of your careless attitude, missing the obvious. Why did you not even want to hear the side of the two girls in addition to Yatola and her friends' version before deciding?

Mandy's mum calculated her potential losses and found a quick way out. She found a new place for Mandy and transferred her to Charles Dickens. She banned her from ever associating with Zena.

You wrote to the home manager calling for a school case conference to discuss Zena's current suspension and behaviour. It was a summary meeting. Yatola and her friends weren't even there. You simply told Zena's carers that you could not tolerate her behaviour and would not accept her back.

Would that have been a satisfactory closure if Zena and Mandy had been your daughters?

Now we reinterpret what happened in your office on this Easter Monday. The world has waited for three years to have some justice for you. That never came. So that was just a reminder of the existing anger in people for your siding with some old pupils against a newcomer. You persecuted Zena just because she was a looked after child, and she tried to stand up against bullies. Did you or the class teacher give her a chance to say a word? No. Did the other ones have that chance? Plenty. Yatola went veveveve…yea. Nonstop. You never once raised a finger to stop her. She even swore and spat at Zena while Mandy and the other three girls watched. Who did you blame everything on? Zena. You threatened to sack Mandy's mum for having tried to help a hapless girl settle down in a volatile class. Mandy's mum ended up moving her daughter to another school, much to Mandy's unhappiness.

Although some people are in power, they probably are nothing more than loud mouths with blind eyes. Did you know that Mandy's stepdad threatened to send her back to the Philippines if she maintained interacting with Zena? New marriage, new job, new school for Mandy, and of course, a new girl on the block. You threatened all these. What options did you leave Mandy's mum?

Kitty, you basically taunted Zena for having unacceptable street behaviours; you taunted her just for being in care. Now you wondered why your office was smashed. Of course, the two wrongs have not made a right yet.

Zena was permanently excluded on the grounds of having told the class teacher that she had no chance to say her side of the story. She had been punished for trying to be helpful, something that should have revealed the vile behaviour of Yatola and her three friends. While I can offer apologies for the innocent school kids, I must say that you deserve being fired for discriminating against children in care.

Did you not know that like every child, especially those of us in care, the school is the most important establishment after our own family home? The school gives friends, knowledge, and even caring adults who keep no grudges and are willing to listen. That picture is messed up by people like you who pick on them just because they are in care. Talk of blind stereotyping by someone who is supposed to be an educator! Did someone forget to tell you that you are supposed to help your staff make school a positive experience for children? Maybe you should consider looking for a job in a different industry, Mrs Skinner, an industry that has nothing to do with children.

You told Zena the killer phrase that mortifies every child in care: "I know your history and we're having no discussion. You are nothing but a trouble maker."

Now listen, Kitty. As for the smell you suffered from the special parcel in your drawer, here is something for your ears only. Let me whisper into your ears: "We ain't bovvered. We aaain't bovvvered!" I hope you heard me.

How can Looked-after-Children ever trust teachers, when heads like you, who should have been motherly, cannot understand? Is it any wonder that some daughters are off the rails, given these models of fairness?

Mrs. Kitty Skinner, we are like any other children. We too have dreams. We like learning and want to be included in activities and enjoy school. We want to join in, make friends, do well, and celebrate our successes. We also come in varieties, moving between what one would call normal balanced family homes all the way to disturbed ones where even cats lack a moment's sleep. To teach us effectively, you need to find out what we like and treat each of us as an individual. Take the effort to positively understand and boost our motivation and willingness to make the best of our present, and write off our disturbed past. Only then can we experience as high academic achievements as any other children.

At times, you get joy by giving up looking for it, just as a butterfly lands on your finger when you have stopped chasing it and are relaxed. That applies to you, Mrs. Kitty Skinner. If you stop treating us as if we are guilty, then you can learn to see our sweet side. Our goodness shall come flowing to you.

You need to help us learn by making learning fun and desirable. Mary Poppins shall tell you that a spoonful of sugar helps the medicine go down in a most delightful way. She reminds you that if you put an element of fun in any job to be done, the job is game, and every task you undertake becomes a piece of cake. Even a robin knows that a song will move any job along. Yes a song, not tears, will move learning along.

So, dear madam head, dear Kitty, you may want to suspend your judgment and negative expectations of children in care. Give us a chance to have a normal school life and believe that behaviour can be modified quicker with a dose of love and honey.

Many of you who cannot teach well, at times, want to find scapegoats. Who is easier to blame than looked after children? After all, failed placements seem to always blame them. Maybe we children should also talk about data protection. I have heard about it but do not really know how it works. Maybe we should be asked how much you teachers can know about our past and decide what to allow and what not to allow.

While you are told our history, including any learning problems, in good faith, many of you become prejudiced and expect too little in the way of our performance. On the contrary, you are quick to anticipate and accept misbehaviour allegations of a pupil in care. You forget that if this child was yours, or it was you in her shoes, you would have been pleading for understanding.

Many of your kind only keep in contact with social workers and carers to report problems while not really helping with organising and managing homework difficulties. You ignore carers' letters asking for suggestions on how to help us LACs with homework, but you are quick to write to carers about an impending exclusion, ticking all forms to cover your back.

We only want to learn. We have enough problems behind us. We only want support and guidance to move forward. When we misbehave, it is rarely the head of year or head of school who has the personality and mellow charm to talk to a disturbed and angry child. Find that person among the teachers and let that one talk us through our issues. For a drop of honey, as my mum told me, catches more flies than a gallon of poison.

As for you Kitty, being "a kitty skinner," you may go and continue skinning your cats, another cruel act much to the wrath of the animal lovers. Will someone get this woman out of education establishments, and certainly out of our schools, please? We need positive experiences from school.

Under the same maturing thought, it took us a long time, discussing, and arguing with my friend Laura. The major question was what risk we ran if we apologized to you for what happened a year ago. Well, we did ask, Shall we apologise to Mrs. Kitty Skinner? The answer was yes.

Now here is a surprise for me, every reader, and Mrs Skinner. We apologise deeply for having been dragged down to such a lowly level in trying to get even with you. In hindsight, we realize that by giving in to the temptation of revenge, we became as bad as you. We could have been better. Now we certainly know better and shall be better people than you. Actually, if I fail to become a medical doctor, I shall deliberately become a teacher. I mean to make a better teacher, a model teacher to both other teachers and students. I shall give every child a chance to shine. If I ever become a school head, I shall ensure that the background of a child is never fully revealed to any teacher, so as to avoid prejudices.

Tell us then, Kitty, would it not be easier to teach all kids as if they came from the same family and give them all the same royal attention that princes and princesses receive? What child would ever resist such treatment? Certainly not me. I know that approach works, as I have repeatedly reminded you about Mr Size.

We, children in care, want to be treated as living individuals and not cases. Certainly not as nut cases. Be it in school or in the social care environment, we deserve the same amount of commitment and attention your biological children receive in your own homes. Why, I wonder, do planners think we deserve less, just for being in care? What is our sin that we committed when we were consigned to this state of nonentity?

We want to be helped, to grow, and to learn. Yes, nurture and nature differ, in reality and not just on paper. It is the same yearning that I expressed to my boyfriend Greg. I really wish his parents would look at me as their future daughter-in-law from now on and not look at my sad past. What use is my past? Who saws sawdust, Mrs Skinner? So why were you torturing Zena for her past, whose real story you hardly knew?

Well, we feel sorry for ourselves. However the bottom line is that we shall strive to make better adults than you. We are really sorry that we had to act so poorly before realizing that we could rise above your petty nastiness. We are sorry for all children who may have heard about our behaviour and believed we were getting even. For, as my Dad repeatedly said, you can never really get even. You can become as bad as the perpetrator, and so be the worst loser as you lose your good character, or you can become a winner by rising above the rotten state of your victimizer.

Now do I understand the folly of a tooth for a tooth.

Here is a word of reminder to all those like Mrs Skinner. If you suspend your pride, you can have one lesson or two plus a free ride. Who is best to advise you about catching a criminal than an ex-con? If you want to teach us successfully and enjoy your job, much as we want to enjoy learning, the following are methods that none of us would resist.

Praise and encourage us, rather than criticize us. Using the word *and* instead of *but* will make your criticism effective, without us feeling criticized.

Tell us exactly and clearly what you want us to do, and do not tell us just what *not* to do, for the most broken and defied commandments start with "shall not."

Look for ways to catch us doing right and then shower us with praise and accolades. We shall bend backwards to live up to your expectations. With relaxed, but loving posture, come closer to us when you want to get our attention.

We expect you to be able to play both child and adults. So do please come down to our level at times and involve us in a non-official capacity. Only then, can we let our guards down and let you into our guarded personalities, which you can then stealthily help us to improve.

Really, you could help us become sensitive, caring, intelligent individuals as we grow by simply incorporating play in every possible aspect of our development.

There was no way I would have stayed in my infant school if my teachers had never let me play in the first months. They even used toys to make me start learning without attracting my attention to the fact. For example, I learned more about triangles from cutting cakes than I did from the books. Pure common sense.

We want love and to be sensitive to others' feelings. We want to make friends and be loved in society. Keeping us on our guard against possible accusations and misunderstandings does not help us build our self image. So help us with empathy and our faces shall give you a smile that can accompany you for a good night's sleep.

Do you want more revolutionary facts, Mrs. Skinner?

Most children in care are geniuses waiting to blossom in some area, celebrities being held back by society. Subsequently, we may be emotionally and socially less mature than our actual ages. Yet we often are full of life, enthusiastic, active, and often passionate. We are burning with possibilities that we wish we had been helped to realize. Hence, our negative behaviours demand your calm and patient understanding, trying as we may be.

These burning possibilities, at least for me and my friend Laura, seem to create so much confusion that we can see ourselves having split attention. For us, you never issue multiple orders, for we only remember and execute the last. You may tell me to wash the dishes, put the laundry on the line, and water the flowers, as you go to town for shopping. I definitely will have watered the flowers and then gone off to my room to listen to music or read a Mills and Boon. I am at the mercy of total distraction. No offence intended. You must give me one step instructions or write them down so I can tick off what I have finished as I go.

Similarly, just as you give us a time table, many of us want some predictable structure. When we know the routine, we can slowly ease from one activity into another. Any abrupt moves upset us. Is it any wonder then that you find us appearing difficult when we have been moved to a new school? Or that many of the children show negative behaviour when staff members leave?

Change is unsettling to many of us children. I shall only know how you adults respond to change when I become one of you. I may look like I am reacting to you, being stroppy about you, but I am actually resenting the change I am going through. I am scared of the unknown immediate and distant future. You need the presence of mind to avoid swallowing hook, line, and sinker, and unleashing your venom of reprimands and exclusions as a reaction to my behaviour.

Isn't it surprising that you adults never think of preparing us children gradually for a planned change? I hear that someone likened bringing successful change to creating various shapes of ice. I can't remember the details, but it was something along the lines of not smashing ice with a hammer, but unfreezing it first, till the water becomes shapeless. Then, you put it in a desired mould and then refreeze it in the plate. Presto! You have ice in the shape you desired. But unless you keep it in a reinforced state of ice, it may freeze back.

Talking of reinforcements, each child has an area of strength, which if identified, praised, and amplified shall actively replace the negative areas. Too many times even the child is not aware of these areas. It took a chance insistence from my private tutor for me to discover that I can draw and paint wonderfully.

One day, he realized that I was angry and burning with some issues that had gone on over the weekend. I simply could not concentrate on his lessons. He gave me a clean pad with lots of papers in it, gave me red, blue, and black pens and a pencil, and asked me to make myself a coffee and draw whatever I wanted.

At first I told him that I could not. But when he insisted, I told myself that drawing whatever I wanted was a much better option than solving simultaneous equations. I surprised myself with the results as I had managed to draw the church that stands on the corner of the road leading to my mum's house. I had done it with so much detail, as if I had the real building in from of me. In reality, the church was at least a hundred and fifty miles away.

Now I have a stash of pencils, crayons, and pads for drawing and painting whenever I am bored. You can guess my next target: try bigger ones and take them for exhibitions.

Do I regard myself as an artist? No. If it was not for my tutor's positive channelling, would the artist in me have stood up? No. He used the trick to enable me to unwind, and it did more than just unwind me. He made the real talented me stand up and be counted.

Forget about conventional punishment. We have suffered so much before that any more negativity from any authority is an expected abnormality. Better fight our weaknesses by showing us overwhelming goodness. Soon, goodness becomes catchy, and we shall not only blush for misbehaving but move the earth to show that we are internally good.

I hope that Mrs. Kitty Skinner is reading this, or at least someone may recognize the plot and tell her about our remorse.

You see, I listen and take advice. Having tried everything, it is only the thought of Angela, the most motherly care worker, and Mr. Size, the one in a million teacher, that I have been feeling very guilty about fags, skunk, and all that. It is now three weeks since my last fag and three months since I touched weed. I vow never to do it again. But such is the effect of love from a caring teacher, Mr. Size, whom I saw years ago.

And another thing. Like I told Miss Fox, you may want to remember this. While ever chided children chase chuff, ever praised paupers pick prizes.

On behalf of the Zenas, Lauras, and Taxies of this world, children in care or looked after children, children on the fence, I send you my love, nonetheless.

Taxie. XXX

CHAPTER 16

Fostering the World's Most Loving Kids

Candle Mews,
Radnor-cliff crescent
Folkestone,
CT20 2JQ

Today' s date

Dear Miss Fox,

You have been long coming. We have been expecting you, but can you keep a secret?

Did I hear that you are bubbling with love, sizzling with the rare virtue of patience, power your cooker with imagination, have endurance for your pillow, and inspiration as your living assistant? Yes, you must be one of the people we, the looked after children, have been looking for everywhere! Welcome Miss Fox. Do please come in.

Sit yourself down, and make yourself at home. Yes, I have been burning with anticipation. The enthusiasm of seeing you and talking to you about my experiences and the secrets I discovered about being a successful foster parent have been my shadow. I cannot wait to start talking, but I must ensure that you are listening. Grab yourself a cup of coffee. Or is it tea you prefer?

So where shall we start then? Where to find the children the kind of a home we want? Or to make you comfortable shall we take away your fears and show you what dreams we have and what we can bring to you? Later, shall we deal with the horror stories you no doubt have heard about challenging behaviours? Well, operating from dreams and observing successful placements, I hope I shall also show you how to have Christmas every day while others wring their hands in anguish at failing placements.

Deal or no deal, Miss Fox? Deal. Okay, then we needed you, Miss Fox. You mean the world to us, as everyone like you is a lifeline for some child. You can take it from me, I am one of the looked after children, in flesh and blood.

Fostering can be child's play and a joy never to be found elsewhere. We would give away the whole world, just to have you. You have been scared by horror stories, I know. But now hear the truth, straight and warm, directly from the horse's mouth. Every child who has ended up under some supervision order always wishes for two things, and no more.

She wishes that everything that happened was not real, that very soon she will be returning to her sweet home where everyone laughs excitedly at the reunion.

She also wishes that if what happened is real, then someone more than a fairy shall lovingly and kindly come to offer her a loving foster home and adoption.

Soon thereafter, the only wish that remains a near dream is the last one. As one is kept in the residential home and sees others being picked to sample and ultimately settle in a foster family, one hopes one's turn is next.

To be honest, Miss Fox, remaining in the children's residential home hurts. Even after only one other child has left into foster care, it hurts. It feels like being on the dance floor with others, and having everyone else be asked to dance except you. Worse still that feeling wells up each time you see, hear, or talk about someone who has moved into a foster family. "Why not me?" I ask, often crying myself to sleep.

Waiting to be fostered is like being on the fence of a house with a birthday bash. You may be near the house, yet you cannot go in. You desperately wait for someone to invite you in. Can you feel the feeling? I am one of those children on the fence. I have been there for the last three years now, and it feels like a century.

Now Miss Fox, can you keep a secret? Promise you are going to keep this secret. I, like all children I guess, fear being ridiculed if others should discover my secrets. Just to show you how important your fostering is to us, I shall let you in into the top ten dreams of a child on the fence.

1. To find some loving and patient family that shall be the first and last foster home.
2. To go into some loving kind, patient, and appropriate foster family willing and able to meet my special needs.
3. To prove lovable, acceptable, and joy-bringing to the foster family and to avoid multiple placements, which interfere with normal development into a confident, responsible adult.
4. That there are sufficient caring individuals and families to make proper foster-child matching and appropriate placements possible.
5. That those of us with siblings shall be placed with more experienced caring fosterers willing to keep siblings together and make that placement our one and only.
6. To meet confident carers who are willing to look beyond our failures, to out-love our past hurts and dented memories, and to help us build our lives.
7. That local authority and council bosses learn to seek third opinions before meddling with our foster caring, before believing that they know what's in a child's best interest without consulting that child.
8. To see our drug driven, lovelorn, love spurned, emotionally-

brainwashed, addict parents assisted to graduate permanently and take us, their children, back in.

9. To see our separating and divorcing parents wise up to the personalities and irreplaceable goodness that they initially enjoyed in each other when they first met and to see them use those as a strength from which to work at their differences.

10. Those of us with no fit home to return to dream of a loving foster family with understanding relatives and a community that can promote our being nurtured beyond fostering onto adoption.

I urge you to re-read our list of dreams, Miss Fox. They tell you about our innermost yearnings, dire necessities, and how important any one person, like you, can be in our lives.

Just in case no one mentioned it to you, some assessment serves to establish whether you are a suitable carer and provides you with all the available information about me as a prospective foster child. You need to have that information so that you can decide if I am the type of child you are willing to have and what type of fostering you are willing to provide.

So, let us assume that you have undergone the usual assessments, ticked all the boxes, and examined the implications on various aspects of your life according to the forms. Let us also assume that you have asked all the relevant questions, including those regarding training. You may already have joined the fostering network. Well then, let me focus on practical approaches and strategies to understand us, help us bring out our inner joys, and realise the success of our dreams.

While I know that you have a heart of gold and cannot wait to receive your first foster child, please heed a few words of caution about your family life. Have you thought about the possible impact fostering can have on your family? We children can put a strain on your existing marriage. I know about a family that took in Harry for fostering. If you thought Henry the Horrid was just a fictional character, you should have met Harry. The stress he brought to the Green family was enough to break it.

As an observer, I noticed a few secret points where the Greens went wrong. After seeing my own parents sail the rocky waters, the problems are now very familiar. Shall I let you in on my other secrets? I have rephrased my observations into ten positive commandments of fostering alongside marriage.

1. Get all of the child's behavioural history so as to set proper rules and boundaries to protect your family. Nip any inappropriate behaviours from us foster children in the bud.
2. If you feel like arguing and disagreeing with one another, do so well away from the kids, so we don't suspect a divided kingdom. Project that you are in control even when you are stressed.
3. Maintain your needs as before and stay young. Keep your hobbies and normal lifestyle, including eating out with friends. That is also a way to teach us how society works, even with the annoying stresses of life.
4. Remember that you are helping us and that you were an established couple when we came, so keep your separate time, as any healthy family would. We can only have successful relationships if we witness you making yours happy.
5. We bring behaviours for which none of your family members are to get grief.
6. Sing from the same hymn book with your husband, checking our claims with each other. That way, we shall have no room to pit one of you against the other.
7. Just as I am standing on the fence crying for the help of a stable, consistent home, you too must seek your own help whenever necessary.
8. Speak out clearly to your spouse about your pressures, needs and feelings.
9. Keep your old friends in the loop. You need them to vent to.
10. Weigh and act on friends' meaningful advice; don't just tire them with your moans.
11. Get all behavioural history so as to make proper rules and

boundaries in protecting your family. Nip any inappropriate behaviour in the bud early.

12. If you feel like arguing and disagreeing, do so well away from the kids, so we don't suspect a divided kingdom. Remain in control even when you are stressed.

13. Maintain your needs as before and keep young. Keep those hobbies and your normal lifestyles, such as eating out with friends. That is a way of teaching us how society works even with the annoying stresses of life.

14. Remember you are helping us and you were already an established couple when we came, so keep your separate time as any healthy family would. We can only have successful relationships if we witness you making your relationships happy.

15. We bring behaviours for which none of your family members should experience grief.

16. Sing from the same hymn book with your husband, checking our claims with each other. That way we shall have no room to pitch you one against the other.

17. Just as I am standing on the fence crying for the help of a stable, consistent home, you too must seek your own help when necessary.

18. Speak out clearly to your spouse about your pressures, needs, and feelings.

19. Keep your old friends in the loop. You need them to vent and talk to.

20. Weigh and act on the meaningful advice of friends and do not just tire them with your moans and complaints.

Now let's address fostering the likes of Taxina, me, who is still on the fence awaiting a loving invitation, despite having challenging behaviours. My chances are blocked by the stereotypes; the negative labels that I get. To be honest, Miss, my bark is probably worse than my bite. I may look and sound like a little dare devil and a damning demon, but deep down, I am a little angel crying out for acceptance. I am a little darling daring to love and be loved, but I just don't know how to go about it the right way.

I can assure you, Miss Fox, that fostering a child with so-called challenging behaviour is not anywhere near as scary as many describe it. Each behaviour is actually a message that has probably taken a wrong delivery method. It is the role of a loving adult to identify this and help children channel their feelings, thoughts, and fears in the appropriate way.

Anyone can uncover the clues by keeping in mind that we may be upset by the immediate environment, the preceding communication or incident. Sometimes it's the situation at hand or even psychological reasons beside the physical ones.

Through challenging behaviour, we can push the boundaries of your emotional resources and management skills. Yet who can best advise you than me, one of the culprits? You need to show the child how to cope with or handle uncomfortable circumstances in ways that help the child settle down and interact positively.

We all need good social skills and relationships with others, even as children, to make friendships, share little secrets, and find someone to talk to when sad and crying.

There are children who click positively with others, managing their feelings well, feeling accepted and valued. These children have positive self-esteem and confidence. Then there are the lot of us who struggle to create, let alone maintain, positive relationships, and we are unhappy. We all want to be like the former. Will you please nurture, support, and promote our social skills and relationships?

You can influence our behaviours by closely watching the way we approach and interact with peers and adults. We become particularly disoriented and upset when arriving in new environments. I guess the case is the same if one moves into a new residential home or foster family. It was challenging and emotional for me living away from my family in circumstances I did not choose.

By being receptive to our needs, being available to children at these times, you shall help us ease into play with others and express our needs and wants appropriately. Gradually, help us to settle down.

Watch for signs of self isolation or becoming withdrawn and avoiding positive interaction with others. That is for me, and many other children I know, one of the sure indicators of inner distress. Those of us with challenging behaviours do need extra support in building relationships. Even if we appear to be independent and not seeking your help, we need support in building good relationships with others.

Children with challenging behaviours often like to relate to adults more than those our own age. Yet we are not really in that category and you may need to craftily tell us to keep out of adult conversations that do not concern us.

It is not that we like interrupting. The reality is that in the new environment, we need a secure attachment with at least one consistent caregiver to enable us to develop social competence and healthy relationships later in life. Yet, not knowing, or deliberately pushing, the boundaries, we may become clingy or possessive about that adult.

In groups, being accepted is necessary for us, but it can create conflicts as well, especially when one wants to assert one's identity and independence. I am sure that you may recall feeling that way in your own teen years, Miss Fox.

At that time, we become pushy, at least I do. But too many times, I have regretted that after my friends ran away from me and played on their own, I was not quick to understand and control feelings of anger, sadness, jealousy, loss, and disappointment. Therefore, we can only live happily if you help us to learn to understand and respect differences, express ourselves appropriately, show compassion and care for others, and how to negotiate (and if necessary lose) with a handshake, as my father used to say, while settling differences. From then on, we can recognise and empathise with others' feelings and express our own in ways that hurt no one.

I see you start to wring your hands in anguish. No, Miss, there is nothing of rocket science about living with us. We are kids like everyone else is or once was. Our only difference is that we need help to unclutter our brains and relate without experiencing prejudice.

Judging from how Angella (one of my elderly carers who I shall miss forever) treated me, it takes nothing unusual.

Keeping in mind that most of us children on the fence and experience constant feelings that the odds are stacked against us, there are obvious triggers that other people consider to be of no importance. We can, therefore, be upset by boredom which translates into a search for excitement; noisy environments, especially when the noise is sudden; feelings of frustration at the lack of or limited communication; feelings of being ignored, oppressed or targeted by others; and the fear of overcrowded places in which we feel threatened by strange faces, and even seemingly unwanted interaction with others when we want to be left alone.

Of course, we can equally get upset under the influence of drugs, or (as according to our assessment) inappropriate responses to our requests and expectations. The absence of clear rules, positive reinforcement and reassurance in new environments do not help the cause.

These triggers do not exclude physical causes such as exhaustion, physical illness, emotional upheavals such as bereavement or even the departure of some carer to whom I may have been attached. However, as always, prevention is better than a cure.

You can anticipate challenging behaviours and intervene in time if you observe the tell-tale signs such as pacing about, increased rate of breathing, tense muscles and clenched fists, and in some cases, even facial expressions.

Introduce some favourable structures and divert our attention to preferred activities, while ignoring the negative direction.

Similarly, you can reduce our anxiety by keeping us well informed in all plans that concern us. Better still, involve us in the planning, or do let us plan ourselves, and just guide us. That way, we have no one to suspect of secret plans. If you replace the behaviour with some functional alternative such as a game of basketball, you enable us to learn substitution as a coping strategy.

In designing the consequences, you need to be creative. Consistency is the word. That's what leads to a positive and productive attitude. Plan a regular strategy and positive interactions that clearly indicate that you hate the behaviour, not the child. Over time, the child shall be too ashamed to let you down and will slowly stop the behaviour.

Patiently wait for the moment to catch your child doing right and sing her praises all evening. Then, use it as a launching pad to communicate your expectations and create joint rules and routines. This way, you exaggerate the strengths and minimize the weaknesses. I have yet to see a child who does not warm up to praise, including yours truly, Taxine.

To sum it up, remember the ABC steps.

A is the analysis of what preceded the outburst.

B is the actual behaviour that has been shown and needs to be changed.

C is the consequence you need to creatively craft, hopefully jointly with my input so that I own up and make it work.

Spot the exact behaviour to be changed. Look for the antecedent in terms of the preceding events, exact time, frequency, any company or lack of it and part of the day, if relevant. You may have to chart the behaviours over some weeks and analyse them. This information helps you plan a working consequence.

The consequence must be a planned change. Choose the most

appropriate time and involve me, the child, in setting the goals. I have heard this referred to as child-focused fostering, Miss Fox. Let the child make all decisions, (well, actually, make the child believe she does) about the short and long term goals, the people to be involved and what exactly will happen. If the child sees the plan as her own, even if you have been steering it, the outcome is likely to be more successful.

Be specific in your plan. For example, Taxine shall do her homework quietly and finish it by nine o'clock. Specify in-built forward moving rewards as well. For instance, when four outstanding behaviours occur, Taxine shall have surprise free time or go to watch a movie of her choice. Let the rewards change as the child grows.

Trust us, give us a good name, and we shall walk the world to prove we can behave. Yes pretty much as quoted in *Oliver Twist*: "I shall do anything, anything, anything for you."

Naturally, in the spirit of child-focused fostering, all decisions are being taken in the best interest of the child, in partnership with the child and her advocates, and are communicated to the family. Knowing that one's progress is being acknowledged by many significant people improves the self esteem of the child and promotes the feelings of being in positive touch and securely related to the people in one's network. Well it does for me, anyway. Also, it reinforces my self-worth as I want all the people to know that I am being good.

You telling others about the goodies that Taxina has been doing warms me up and helps me outgrow the victim/villain label of "trouble maker" or "ever dependent attention-seeking child." I slowly begin to believe in myself, developing such resilience as to try and deal with life's adversity. I feel supported and begin to feel control over my own life. You can now see why I said you count a million times by just being there. You are the base of my resilience. Your patience, endurance, and shrewd calculation of when to time yourself out as I seem to push boundaries too much are all ingredients.

Your focusing on my strength and letting my failings fade away in the distance is a loud statement about my positive value. As I develop a positive attitude, confidence, and self esteem, I develop the strength to begin to relate sensibly to adults and other children. I learn to communicate properly with stability and self control.

If I can achieve these short-term goals, I can confidently face the future head-on, without any fear. I can plan my future goals and how I will achieve them. I can slowly self-direct. The beginning may be the rocky tantrums about which I am now terribly ashamed, but with you by my side, I slowly realize that any dream is achievable.

Of course, we need to jointly review how well I am doing in achieving the objectives that make up my goals. Then, we can celebrate my achievements with a week of horse riding, a picnic in the park, or a nice pack of lingerie. We children love gifts and rewards, Miss Fox.

I am just one of the children waiting on the fence for a loving foster home. I hope I have calmed your fears. Do please come look around and leave the lemons. Do take your pick.

[As this is my last letter, I would request you dear readers to get back to me with your ideas about any areas that you wished I had addressed. I may be encouraged to write a few more letters to address the shortfalls. So do please write to me about what you liked about this book and where and how you want improvements. Please send your feedback to taxina@greatestcaringsecrets.com.]

For a final morale booster, remember these magic words:

While ever chided children chase chuff,
Ever praised paupers pick prizes.

From the cliff of the singing winds, I send you shiploads of Love,
Taxie XXX

CHAPTER 17

When the Future met the Past

Candle Mews,
Radnor-cliff crescent
Folkestone,
CT20 2JQ

Today' s date

Dear Mothers and Daughters:

To a poetic summary, everything I muse
Dalia had a present, one she did not use

In wrong times and empty places, she looked for love
But love least fought for do men only abuse
Try as she may in past love only she had lost
In lower ranks crashed her one hope
To glide easily tried she bottom power
To win favours from above
But as lust soon wore, in came tears to mope
Written in lines of shame is her past.

Looking to the future, she fears the joy won't last
She has today to sing, dance and choose
Another well training for job, for freedom

But she lives in fears, sees the future in tears
That fast cars crush, was spurned wisdom
Searching endless male attention stole her time
Advising her against it was everyone's crime.

Had her invincible youth when everything is possible
That too as days passed did get lost
She cannot recall when, where or how
Besides a baby, her dreams bore a ghost.
For big money did she try Accounting
With eyes on books and men in mind
Success eluded her, no qualifications could she find
Got a job in a hotel as a maid, it was soon to be said
A super maid, for a room did she pay by guests to be laid.

A ghost haunting past or a smile glaring future?
For having weak roots did the mightiest oak fell
That now matters, that it's a choice may someone tell
Or to Dalia in a song the message sing
Investing in the now for a cheque and a wedding ring
Are possible if you ignore the past, but hold the dream fast
Ask the crying baby or your oldies to tell you how
When boobs sag, and bums slim only brains last

So be humble, listen and learn fast,
For Mary fairies for quick money tried she a life as a wife
But the face is scarred and the beauty gone
For a battering ram was her husband of a heart of stone.

CHAPTER 18

Just One Ear

Candle Mews,
Radnor-cliff crescent
Folkestone,
CT20 2JQ

Today's date

To All Adults who know about fears:

Tears, fears, and ears,
Making Children in Care a Success?
I start my day with a tear
So where is my future?
From the past the future I fear
Someone please help with a listening ear?

Lend me one ear,
If only you could hear,
Way beyond my noise and behaviour of no choice
The attempt to make that a voice
The bleeding of my young heart so dear
As I approach my future in fear
For my tainted past made nothing clear
Of how the future to make a success.

Will you make this trembling person a life success?

If I may count on you
One thing I plead you to do
One ear do please lend me
Listen beyond my tantrums,
Hazy behaviours and my seeming mean
Talk to and not at me is what I mean
Involve me, teach me and help me decide.

Help me; hear me out crying for attention from inside,
So some hope I can see,
Like all others learn to smile if my life can ever be worth awhile
Give me some tip from your experience
As I err, I also want to listen
How beyond my tears to move,
Bigger than my fears myself to prove
With kindness every advice let me be given.

I may pretend not to hear your voice,
Please insist that I have one choice
Which is to listen, learn, and grow
Frustrating but persist for I do want to grow up
To tranquil independence, not a silently regretting voice
I know you are trying, but I need more of your love
And what more I have to return is love, love and love.

Taxina XX

Web Resources

www.change-management-coach.com/kurt_lewin.html

www.change-management-coach.com/kurt_lewin.html

www.communitycare.co.uk/.../2009/.../social-work-practices-for-children-in-care-pilots-set-out-plans.html

www.dcsf.gov.uk/rsgateway/DB/SFR/s000878/index.shtml

http://www.direct.gov.uk/en/Parents/
Adoptionfosteringandchildrenincare/index.htm

www.fosteringresources.co.uk/

www.fostering.net/

http://www.fostering.org.uk/information/default.html

http://www.independent.co.uk/opinion/commentators/rob-williams-why-children-at-risk-are-not-put-into-care-1028132.html

www.independent.co.uk/.../leading-article-children-in-care-deserve-better-419582.html

http://www.sanguineconsulting.com/WorkshopsNew/
challengingbehaviourMEL08.html

www.sehd.scot.nhs.uk/mels/CEL2009_16.pdf

www.bcft.co.uk

www.dailymail.co.uk/news/article-1244699/

www.greatestcaringsecretsrevealed.com (care follow up articles)

www.superfitnessempire.com

About The Author

Francis Epulani a Social Scientist, and a seasoned mentor of children in care, aka looked-after-children, is based in Kent, in the United |Kingdom. , he has also taught extensively in Care Homes for Looked After Children. It is from that work that this book originated, as his contribution to bringing a voice to looked after children. He has worked extensively, managing projects in natural resources and rural livelihoods in Malawi; done ecotourism consultancies in the SADC region.

He was educated at Bunda College, university of Malawi; Wye College, University of London, Birkbeck College Univertsity of London; and Institute of Market Research, Economic Sociology and Agricultural Policy, Bonn University.

He further obtained a postgraduate diploma in Primary Health Care Management and a postgraduate diploma in Leadership and Management from the Institute of Leadership and Management.

A member of the Chartered Institute of Management, Institute of Learning (UK) and the American Consultant's League, Francis Epulani is currently working as a Business Practice Manager, while carrying out management consultancies.